HARMONY KORINE: COLLECTED SCREENPLAYS I

T0322879

HARMONY KORINE
Collected Screenplays

VOLUME I
Jokes
Gummo
julien donkey-boy

faber and faber

This collection first published in 2002
by Faber and Faber Limited
The Bindery, 51 Hatton Garden, London ECIN 8HN

Typeset by Faber and Faber Ltd
Printed and bound by CPI Group (UK) Ltd, Croydon, CRO 4YY

Jokes, Gummo, 'Untitled', *julien donkey-boy,* and Introductions
© Harmony Korine, 2002

Photograph of Harmony Korine by Bruce Birmelin
Still from *Gummo* © Fine Line Features
Still from *julien donkey-boy* © Fine Line Features

A CIP record for this book
is available from the British Library
ISBN 978-0-571-21002-2

FSC
www.fsc.org
MIX
Paper | Supporting
responsible forestry
FSC® C013604

Printed and bound in the UK on FSC® certified paper in line with our continuing
commitment to ethical business practices, sustainability and the environment.
For further information see faber.co.uk/environmental-policy

Our authorised representative in the EU for product safety is
Easy Access System Europe, Mustamäe tee 50, 10621 Tallinn, Estonia
gpsr.requests@easproject.com

23

CONTENTS

Harmony Korine.

INTRODUCTION
by Harmony Korine

charles eames was most notably an architectural engineer, a furniture designer, a man of scientific theory, but most impressive to me were his films – films about toys, spinning tops, toy towns, toy soldiers, toy trains (most famous of the films were his two short masterpieces *powers of ten* and *national aquarium presentation*). he will be remembered first and foremost as a creator of chairs. he did not give philosophical credence to his own separate and varied modes of creation; in essence his chairs and his films were one and the same. the content was king, and thus developed a 'unified aesthetic' that brought the walls down and allowed him to work free of any of the self-imposed constraints that most artists suffer. personally, i have published books of fiction, books of photos, displayed my art in many galleries and in many forms, made recordings of banjo music, written and directed films, composed a symphony using only the same three black keys on the right-hand side of the piano, and i most importantly am now trying to revive the tap-dance scene by developing an entirely new repertoire of semi-improvised, extremely technical, avant-garde dance structures. (please do not think i am joking; it would be of the deepest misunderstanding to interpret my intent, my dream, as somehow being an ironic display. i am admittedly not as advanced at the moment as need to be before i showcase this next phase in my career. if my dream comes to fruition and i am capable of a total tap revolution, then i declare without any hesitation or pause a complete and total abandonment of my current involvement in the cinema and all other areas of artistic contention. i need to go where i am most useful.) the point being: everything from me had been previously deposited inside of me. this is due to the force of a sacred entity whose identity i will take to my grave. this curse/blessing was bestowed upon my being without any previous knowledge and total disregard

of personal choice in the matter, with no consent. and when i
am dead, perhaps I too will be best remembered for a chair i
once built.

Jokes

INTRODUCTION

jokes is a film that i wrote about two years ago. i have always been a fan of vaudeville, and i have for a long time had the desire to direct and revive the classic blackface minstrels of yesteryear, in particular those early al jolson and eddie cantor classics that helped inspire me to become the person i am today. in fact, my two life-long dream projects are both epic in scope: the first is to be a tap-dancing minstrel in a film starring myself called *the grace of blackface*; the other film would be a historical period drama, tracing in great detail the history of molestation in the boy scouts. i would go decade by decade showcasing the most infamous boy-scout molesters of the day. i would focus particularly on the evolution of the scout-master molester, how with each passing era the methods and sophistication would increase accordingly, in essence becoming more and more uniformly perverse, reflecting the times and attitudes of the day, and ending up with the common flat-out pedophilic mantra that is the boy scouts of america. in fact i have already been working on a script that combines both themes, a period minstrel drama about the history of boy-scout molesting. but *jokes* is a separate undertaking, written in conjunction with the former. it is a movie in three parts. each chapter so to speak is based on a milton berle joke, usually a one-liner in the vein of henny youngman. basically i picked three separate jokes and embellished each one in order to stretch out a simple narrative of sorts. at the time i was watching all the alan clark films i could see and i was very much excited by his technique, his use of long flowing steady cam, no frills organic filmmaking. so i was inspired to approach each joke/chapter in a similar way, a return to a place i had never before felt any interest.

The title 'Jokes' appears on an all-black screen. The letters are spelled out in an old-fashioned font.

Credits roll on top of wildly zany circus music. An orchestra of kazoos and strange harps.

As soon as the credits finish the screen goes to black.

We hear the voice of Mugsy, a sensitive-sounding man in his mid-thirties.

MUGSY (V.O.)

> He used to date a schoolteacher. Every time he wrote her a love letter, she sent it back corrected.

INT. INDOOR POOL – DAY

Mugsy and Karen are both albinos. They are standing in the shallow end of the swimming pool throwing a small red beach ball back and forth. Karen is wearing a blue swimsuit with an American flag printed on top of the bosom area. Mugsy has a dirty blue cast on his left arm.

The word 'EASTER' appears at the top left-hand corner of the screen.

Other people, mostly adults, are swimming around doing laps.

Mugsy and Karen are a married couple in their early to mid-thirties. They both have completely white hair and skin. Their wintery blue eyes provide the only color on their body.

A few people are lined up on the diving boards at the other end of the pool.

The loud sound of water splashing and voices echoing is heard.

Mugsy and Karen giggle like children as they toss the ball back and forth to one another.

INT. USED RECORD/COMIC-BOOK STORE — DAY

Karen and Mugsy are standing in the middle of the store looking at records.

They are both wearing matching black baseball jackets with Janet Jackson T-shirts underneath. Mugsy is wearing a red baseball cap with his name embroidered on it in large white letters.

The store is huge and people of all ages are walking around searching through the aisles.

Karen pulls out an album with Prince on the cover. It has a picture of him sitting on a unicorn almost completely naked except for a torn towel wrapped around his waist.

> KAREN

Look, Mugsy.

> MUGSY

What?

> KAREN

I've never seen this Prince album.

Mugsy looks over.

> MUGSY

Is he on a horse?

> KAREN
> *(laughing to herself)*

It's a unicorn.

Mugsy turns his head and continues flipping through the records.

Karen sticks the Prince album back in.

Mugsy stops flipping and pulls out a Gladys Knight and the Pips album.

> MUGSY

My grandmother's name was Gladys.

He sticks the album in front of Karen's face.

KAREN

It was?

MUGSY

Like Gladys Knight and the Pips.

KAREN

I've never heard you talk about her.

MUGSY

She died when I was boy.

Karen stares at the cover of the album.

It's funny, my grandmother was a great singer in her own
right. She wasn't famous, but in our family she was
famous for her singing voice.

KAREN

You wanna get the album then? It's got a 99-cent sticker.

MUGSY

Yeah, we probably should.

Mugsy smiles and then tucks the album firmly under his arm.

INT. CHURCH – EVENING

*A black preacher with golden eye glasses is screaming out the words
to a gospel song. He is clapping his hands together and stomping his
left foot up and down on the stage.*

*A small band of musicians is playing behind the black preacher. The
members are all dressed casually in blue jeans and sweaters.*

*A thirteen-year-old black boy in a three-piece suit is playing the
drums.*

*Karen and Mugsy are standing up along with the rest of the congre-
gation.*

*The two of them are in the middle of the church swaying back and
forth with their hands sticking straight up above their heads.
Mugsy's red hat is sitting upside down on the pew.*

The room is about one quarter of the way full with an assortment of odd-looking characters, all of them singing, many of them holding hands.

A fat woman with a polka-dot blouse and a nose ring is holding a wooden crutch high above her head.

Karen has her eyes shut.

Mugsy is singing very loudly and snapping his head back and forth like a person slightly possessed.

The thirteen-year-old drummer boy twirls the drum stick around in his hand and then bangs down on the brass cymbal.

INT./EXT. CAR – NIGHT

Mugsy is driving a small red 1983 Toyota.

Karen is sitting quietly on the passenger side. They both have their seat belts on.

The radio in the car looks like it has been stolen because wires are sticking out of the slot where the radio should be. Rain begins to drizzle onto the windshield.

                         KAREN
          You should turn on the wipers, Mugsy.

Mugsy clicks the windshield wipers on.

Karen picks up a crumpled napkin from off the floor and wipes some dust off the dashboard.

She sticks the napkin in her coat pocket.

INT. RESTAURANT – NIGHT

Close-up of Mugsy. He is holding his breath and his face has turned a strange color purple.

His cheeks are almost bursting from the pressure.

Mugsy and Karen are sitting opposite one another at a large checkerboard dinner table.

Karen is looking down at her bulky black calculator wrist watch.

In one mighty burst Mugsy exhales and a tad of spittle floats from his lips onto the table top.

> KAREN
> *(still looking at her watch)*
> One minute twenty-three seconds.

Mugsy smiles as the color in his face quickly turns back to its natural white.

> MUGSY

Almost a record.

> KAREN

I wish you'd stop doing that. It looks disgusting. It looks like your head's going to pop. Your head looks like a grape when you do that.

Karen has a glass of ice tea in front of her with a huge lemon wedge hanging off the corner of the glass.

The restaurant is your basic family-style diner.

> MUGSY

I almost broke the record.

Karen makes a face and then unfolds her napkin and places it neatly on her lap.

A skinny waitress with short blonde hair and narrow eyebrows walks up to the table.

Mugsy quickly opens the menu and looks inside.

> SKINNY WAITRESS
> You folks ready to order?

Mugsy closes the menu.

> MUGSY
> *(looking at Karen)*
> You know what you want?

> KAREN

Yes, I would like the pancakes and sausage.

The skinny waitress nods and writes the order down.

> MUGSY

An' all I want is rice pudding and 7 Up please.

The skinny waitress smiles and takes the menus.

> SKINNY WAITRESS

Sure.

Mugsy stares at the skinny waitress as she walks away.

> MUGSY

Do you think she's a lesbian?

> KAREN

Who, the waitress?

> MUGSY

Yeah.

> KAREN

I don't know.

> MUGSY

I think she's probably a lesbian.

> KAREN

Why?

> MUGSY

Her hair was short . . .

> KAREN

So.

> MUGSY

And the way her face looked was exactly like the way a lesbian's face usually looks.

> KAREN

I couldn't tell.

MUGSY

It's strange, but to me all lesbians look a lot alike. They have the same type of face and hair.

KAREN

Short hair.

MUGSY

I remember being in the fifth grade. I had a lesbian math teacher who had hair on the tip of her tongue.

Karen giggles.

KAREN

When I was younger I used to know a lesbian couple.

MUGSY

You did?

KAREN

I used to live next to these two old lesbians. They kept a middle-aged border who was a camp counselor at some sailing camp on the Chesapeake bay. Once I walked by his window and heard a song by the band Queen. And when I looked in his window I saw him totally naked, lying on a bed with his legs spread. He had a cigar in his mouth and he was chewing on the tip of it. I stood there and watched the guy for a while, until one of the old lesbians yelled out at me, 'Quit spyin' on the house guests, that's an invasion of privacy.' I said, 'But hey, the guy's naked.' And she said, 'So what, we're all born naked.'

Mugsy starts giggling.

Karen pops her eyes out and then sips on her drink.

MUGSY

That's when you were how old?

KAREN

I was sixteen then.

MUGSY

That's a funny memory.

KAREN

Yeah.

Mugsy sticks his fork inside his cast and starts itching it back and forth.

He stands up and puts the fork back on the table.

MUGSY

I gotta use the bathroom.

Karen nods and then looks out the window.

Mugsy walks away.

INT. RESTAURANT BATHROOM – NIGHT

Mugsy walks into a small one-stall bathroom with a single urinal.

He steps up to the urinal and takes a piss.

He flushes, then backs away to make sure no one is sitting in the stall.

He pulls a blue magic marker from out of his front pant pocket.

He begins to write on the side of the stall. He does this quickly and his handwriting is extremely messy.

When he's finished the wall reads: IF JESUS WAS A JEW THEN WHY DID HE HAVE A PORTA RICAN NAME?

He sticks the marker back into his front pant pocket and grins wildly at the sentence.

He sticks his middle finger inside his cheek and then makes a loud popping noise with it.

He walks out of the bathroom.

INT. RESTAURANT – NIGHT

Mugsy returns and the food is on the table.

Karen is eating her pancakes.

Mugsy sets his napkin in his lap and begins eating his rice pudding.

INT. VIDEO RENTAL STORE — NIGHT

Mugsy and Karen are standing in the comedy section of the video rental store.

Karen is holding a box of the movie When Harry Met Sally *in her hand.*

> KAREN
> This looks funny. *When Harry Met Sally.*

> MUGSY
> What's it called?

> KAREN
> *When Harry Met Sally.*

Mugsy looks at the back of the box.

> MUGSY
> I'm not in the mood for that.

> KAREN
> You're not?

> MUGSY
> I'm not in the mood for a romantic comedy.

> KAREN
> No?

> MUGSY
> Uh uh.

Karen puts the box back on the shelf.

The two of them continue to scan the racks.

> KAREN
> What are you in the mood for, Mugsy?

MUGSY
Do you want to rent a James Dean movie?

Karen makes a face and shakes her head 'no.'

Two small black girls holding red balloons run down the aisle.

You don't want to watch a James Dean one?

Karen shakes her head 'no.'

KAREN
Should we just get a pornographic movie?

MUGSY
We can always do that.

KAREN
If you want.

MUGSY
(*looking around*)
There's really nothing in this section that interests me.

KAREN
Do you want to rent a pornographic movie?

MUGSY
We can do that.

Mugsy itches his nose with the corner of his cast.

CUT TO:

Mugsy and Karen enter the porno section of the video store.

All the videos are lined up side by side in long rows, with the front of each video facing forward.

A few people, all men, are walking around looking at different titles.

A short old man in a dark green trench coat has a pile of videos in one hand and a white plastic bag in the other.

Mugsy and Karen begin looking.

Mugsy walks down to the far end of the room.

Karen is staring at the different covers.

The old man in the trench coat begins coughing into his hand. He is standing in the gay section. Above his head in electric blue cursive writing is a laminated sign that reads: MEN ON MEN.

Karen turns around and looks at him.

The old man smiles then walks out of the room with his stack of videos.

Karen walks over to where the man was standing and begins to look around.

She picks up a box and smiles. On the cover is a picture of a burly body-builder guy with a Hitler moustache. He is sitting on a red leather couch, completely naked except for a yellow workman's helmet.

Karen takes the box and walks over to where Mugsy is standing.

Mugsy is busy searching out the best porno.

We can hear the sound of kids yelling outside.

Karen walks up behind Mugsy and taps him on the shoulder.

Mugsy turns around.

                          KAREN
We should rent this one.

Mugsy looks at the box. He seems a bit taken aback.

                          MUGSY
This is a gay movie, Karen.

                          KAREN
I know, have you ever seen one?

                          MUGSY
No.

                          KAREN
I figured we could do something unusual for a change.

> MUGSY

Are you sure?

> KAREN

Yeah.

Mugsy looks around to make sure no one is watching them.

> MUGSY

You want to rent a gay movie? There are no girls at all in these movies?

Karen giggles.

> KAREN

I know. We should just get it. It would be something different for a change.

> MUGSY
> (*looking at the back of the box*)

This guy has really big muscles.

> KAREN

I know. I like that.

> MUGSY
> (*smiling and a bit embarrassed*)

You do?

> KAREN

Big muscles make a man look sexy.

> MUGSY

Yeah.

Mugsy looks at Karen and the two of them begin to giggle like children.

INT. MUGSY AND KAREN'S BEDROOM – NIGHT

Mugsy and Karen are side by side riding two separate exercise bikes.

They are both wearing long white night shirts and cheap blue flip-flops. Karen has a pair of yellow headphones on.

The room is fairly large. It is messy, with books and gadgets and clothes thrown all over the place. A collection of vintage Pez dispensers is sitting on a stand near the bed. Their room looks a little bit like Pee Wee's playhouse, except it does have a few traces of adult living. A couple of prescription pill bottles are on the dresser. A large framed photo of Karen and Mugsy sitting together on an elephant is hanging above the bed.

They both continue to pedal.

INT. LIVING ROOM – NIGHT

Mugsy is sitting on the couch with a Casio keyboard on his lap.

There is a small wooden table in front of him with a yellow pad and pencil and a glass of water. A framed jigsaw puzzle of a jet airplane is hanging on the cheap wood-paneled wall behind Mugsy's head.

The television is on a cartoon channel.

All the lights in the room are on.

Karen walks in eating a banana.

Mugsy looks up at her like he's excited.

                    MUGSY
     Turn the volume down.

Karen walks over and turns the television off.

     Don't turn off the set, please. Just the sound.

                    KAREN
     Why?

                    MUGSY
     'Cause I like seeing it in the background when I sing.

                    KAREN
     All right.

Karen turns the TV back on and lowers the sound.

MUGSY

Come sit down.

KAREN

Did you finish writing this song . . .

MUGSY

Yeah.

KAREN

You've been workin' on it for so long.

MUGSY

I just finished it. Come sit down.

Karen walks over and sits down beside Mugsy.

KAREN

What's the name of it?

MUGSY

I'm not sure yet. It's about punk rockers.

KAREN

Like the ones that hang out around the park?

MUGSY

Yeah. I might call it 'Jesus Loves Punkos.'

Karen puts her hand on the back of her head and tries to crack her neck.

KAREN

Yeah.

Mugsy presses a button on the keyboard and then Tchaikovsky's theme to the 'Nutcracker' comes pumping out.

He hits another button and a slow rhythmic waltz comes out.

Mugsy clears his throat and begins to sing. He changes his voice so that it almost sounds like a retarded female opera singer.

> MUGSY
> (*singing*)

Jesus loves punkos oi oi oi, Jesus loves those skinhead
boys, Jesus loves punkos oi oi oi, Jesus loves those skinhead boys. When I was little I used to listen to music. And
there was this guy and he was a preacher with a pole. And
he used to say, so beautifully, he'd say Jesus loves punkos
oi oi oi, Jesus loves those skinhead boys. And heavy metal
kids love Satan man, 666 in the palm of their hands. An'
hyper kids run around on Ritalin, when their parents go
they sip their gin.

*Karen is clapping and moving her shoulders up and down while
holding the half-eaten banana in one hand.*

> (*still singing*)

. . . Jesus loves punkos oi oi oi, Jesus loves those skinhead
boys, Jesus loves punkos oi oi oi, Jesus loves those skinhead boys . . .

Mugsy stops singing and clears his throat.

. . . And it just goes on from there. It just keeps repeating.

Karen smiles and looks proud.

You like it?

> KAREN

Yes, very much.

> MUGSY

You do?

> KAREN

Very much.

The slow waltz on the Casio keyboard continues to play.

INT. KITCHEN – NIGHT

*The house is silent except for the sound of cartoons coming from the
living room.*

Karen is standing by the sink drinking a cup of cocoa. Her hair is pushed back and she looks ready for bed.

She takes a few more sips then empties the rest out in the sink.

She turns the faucet on and rinses off the cup.

She places the cup back into the cabinet.

She yawns.

She walks out of the room and flicks the light off.

INT. HALLWAY — NIGHT

Karen walks through a skinny hallway and clicks the light off.

The sound of the floor creaking is heard.

INT. LIVING ROOM — NIGHT

Mugsy is sitting on the couch with his legs spread.

He is playing with his underarm hair and watching cartoons. The Casio keyboard is resting next to him on the sofa.

Karen walks in.

KAREN
You wanna watch the movie now?

Mugsy looks up.

MUGSY
Yeah. Put it in.

Karen walks over to the television and takes the video out of its container.

KAREN
I confirmed your doctor's appointment for tomorrow.

MUGSY
You confirmed it?

KAREN

Yeah, this afternoon I called.

MUGSY

Good.

KAREN

You can get that dirty cast finally taken off.

She inserts the video into the VCR.

I told 'em to give you a complete check-up. Since it's been I don't know how long since you've last had one . . .

MUGSY

I haven't had a check-up for . . .

KAREN

. . . Five years . . .

MUGSY

. . . Even longer, maybe six or seven years.

KAREN

Well, I'm glad I finally scheduled it.

Karen picks up the keyboard and places it on the floor.

The gay porn begins.

She sits down next to Mugsy and starts to rub his inner thigh.

The cheesy porn music starts in.

Mugsy picks up the VCR remote and fast forwards.

Stop here.

Mugsy presses 'play.'

We see a quick glimpse of the video: two men are tonguing each other while standing under a garden hose.

Mugsy crinkles his eyebrows.

Karen smiles.

                              MUGSY
   Good lord.

Karen giggles.

   That is the biggest penis I have ever seen.

                              KAREN
   Ow my god . . .

                              MUGSY
   It doesn't look real.

The sound of men having sex.

   He has a moustache like Adolf Hitler.

                              KAREN
   It seems so strange to see men like that doing sex.

*She picks up a bottle of skin lotion from off the coffee table and
begins to rub it into the cracks of her toes. Her toenails are colored
bright red.*

                      (*staring at the TV*)
   It looks painful.

                              MUGSY
   His penis looks like it's about ten inches long.

                              KAREN
   Look at how wide it is.

                              MUGSY
   Yeah.

                              KAREN
   It's so wide.

Mugsy looks very interested.

*Another quick glimpse of the video, only now the two men are hav-
ing sex.*

   It looks painful.

Mugsy starts pulling on his underarm hair again.

MUGSY

I think they put oil on themselves to make them look
shiny like that.

KAREN

It is the biggest penis I have ever seen. He looks just like
Burt Reynolds.

*Mugsy looks at the video and smiles in a strange way. It looks like
something has come over him, a peculiar interest.*

Karen looks at Mugsy, who seems a bit transfixed.

Are you disgusted?

Mugsy is silent.

Karen picks up the remote.

Should I shut it off?

MUGSY

No, leave it . . . it's OK.

KAREN

Are you sure?

MUGSY

It's OK.

Karen looks at the TV.

KAREN

He looks just like Burt Reynolds?

*A close-up of the moustachioed man's face on the video. He is
breathing heavily and snorting like a pig.*

EXT. MAGAZINE STAND — DAY

*It is early in the morning and a few people are standing in front of
the magazine rack reading newspapers.*

The wind is blowing.

Mugsy walks up and quickly looks around. He is chewing gum.

He walks over to the porno section and picks up a Playboy *magazine.*

He immediately opens it to the centerfold and begins nodding his head up and down in approval.

He stares at it for a moment then looks around to see if anyone is watching him.

He quickly puts the Playboy *back upside down in its spot.*

He then takes a few steps over to the gay section and begins to pull down magazine after magazine.

He walks up to the man working at the register and pays for a large stack of gay porno magazines.

The man puts the magazines in a brown paper bag.

INT. SWIMMING POOL — DAY

Karen is standing on the edge of the high dive.

She is wearing the same swimsuit from the opening, with the American flag printed on the bosom area. She is also wearing a green shower cap.

She dives head first into the water.

She climbs out of the pool.

She hops up and down on one leg so that the water falls out of her ear.

She pulls the swimsuit wedgy out of her butt.

INT. HOSPITAL HALLWAY — DAY

The hallway is almost completely empty except for a young Spanish boy sitting in a wheelchair next to the water fountain.

He is dipping a plastic comb into the water, then slicking his hair back.

Mugsy is walking down the middle of the hallway with his eyes closed shut and his arms stuck out to the side.

He is walking slowly and clumsily.

After every step he counts out a number. He is trying to count how far he can walk with his eyes closed.

> MUGSY
> . . . nine, ten, eleven, twelve, thirteen, fourteen . . .

He bumps into the wall, then opens his eyes and looks around to make sure no one is watching him.

He smiles embarrassedly at the young Spanish boy, who is still combing his hair back.

A female nurse with a clipboard walks up to Mugsy.

> FEMALE NURSE
> The doctor will see you now.

> MUGSY
> OK.

Mugsy follows the nurse into the doctor's office.

INT. DOCTOR'S OFFICE − DAY

The room is small and bare. The wallpaper is a conservative plaid.

Mugsy is sitting upright on a blue cushioned table.

His shirt and pants are off. He is wearing a pair of tight white Fruit of the Looms. This image is startling because he appears to be completely white. A small portion of his stomach flab is showing.

A tall doctor with a slightly balding mullet hair-do and black Woody Allen spectacles is cutting the cast off of Mugsy's arm. The doctor is wearing a blue suit and sitting on a stool with wheels on the bottom of the legs.

Mugsy looks attentive as the doctor cuts the cast quickly down the center with a large medical scissor.

The cast falls to the floor.

> DOCTOR
> There we go, Mugsy.

Mugsy begins opening and closing his hand.

> How does it feel?

> MUGSY
> Strange. It feels so strange.

The doctor examines his arm.

> DOCTOR
> It seems to have healed well. The bone's adjusted nicely.

> MUGSY
> It feels much lighter.

Mugsy continues to open and close his hand.

CUT TO:

Mugsy is standing up on a scale.

The doctor is weighing him.

> DOCTOR
> You've gained only three pounds.

Mugsy steps off the scale.

CUT TO:

The room is dark.

The doctor is checking Mugsy's ears.

CUT TO:

The lights are back on.

Mugsy is sitting upright on the table.

The doctor is checking Mugsy's heartbeat with a stethoscope.

DOCTOR

Breathe.

Mugsy breathes.

The doctor moves the stethoscope to the other side of Mugsy's chest.

Breathe.

Mugsy breathes.

The doctor slides the stethoscope up close to Mugsy's armpit.

Breathe.

Mugsy breathes.

The doctor stands up and places the stethoscope on Mugsy's back.

Again.

Mugsy breathes.

Deep breath, again.

Mugsy takes a deep breath.

Lean back on the table.

Mugsy lies down flat on his back with his knees sticking straight up.

The doctor scoots his legs down.

He begins to press down on Mugsy's abdomen.

Mugsy looks up at the ceiling and grins.

The doctor shifts his hand to the other side and presses down.

Mugsy dims his eyes a bit.

The doctor slips his hand down Mugsy's underpants and gently grabs his testicles.

Mugsy shuts his eyes and smiles in a relaxed manner.

Cough.

Mugsy is silent.

Cough.

Mugsy says nothing. He only smiles.

Cough.

The doctor keeps his hands in the same spot.

                                        (*louder*)
Mugsy, cough please.

Startled, Mugsy opens his eyes and lets out two deep coughs in a row.

The doctor quickly removes his hand from Mugsy's underpants.

He rolls his chair back a few feet.

He tugs on his earlobe and looks at Mugsy for a slight moment.

I heard a good one the other day.

                         MUGSY
What?

Mugsy pushes himself up.

                         DOCTOR
You can put your pants on. You're perfectly fit.

The doctor stands up and washes his hands in the sink.

A man rushed into the doctor's office and said: 'Doctor, I think I'm going crazy. I have a turnip growing out of my left ear.' 'So you have,' said the amazed doctor, 'how can such a thing happen?' 'I can't understand it,' said the bewildered patient. 'I planted radishes.'

The doctor smiles and winks.

Mugsy giggles.

The doctor wipes his hands off with a paper towel.

Mugsy puts his pants on.

EXT. PARK — DAY

The park is extremely large and spread out.

Mugsy is walking through the grass with his shoes off and pants rolled up to his knees.

He is holding a stack of magazines under his arm. In his other hand he is holding a long piece of purple taffy.

He walks up to a green park bench and sits down on the top of the table.

He takes a bite of the thick taffy and begins to chew it roughly, like a horse.

He opens one of the magazines and starts flipping through pages of naked men.

He stops on one of the pages where a guy who looks just like Fabio is sitting on a fire engine holding his limp, droopy penis.

Mugsy begins to rub the picture.

About a hundred feet away two college-aged boys with their shirts off are throwing a rainbow-colored frisbee back and forth.

Mugsy looks up.

The wind is blowing his hair.

MUGSY

Jesus, I am gay.

Mugsy takes another bite of taffy.

EXT. IN FRONT OF MUGSY AND KAREN'S HOME — DAY

Mugsy drives his car up to the front of his house.

His brakes make a loud squeaking noise.

He jumps out of the car.

He runs up to his front door and enters his home.

INT. MUGSY AND KAREN'S HOME – DAY

Mugsy walks very quickly through the different rooms in his house. He seems extremely serious.

> MUGSY
> (*screaming*)
> Karen! Are you home? Karen! Karen!

He walks through the kitchen and into the living room.

Karen walks in.

Her hair is wet and she is still wearing her bathing suit. She is holding a white towel.

> KAREN
> What's wrong?

> MUGSY
> Karen, sit down.

> KAREN
> Why, what's wrong?

> MUGSY
> Sit down.

> KAREN
> What did the doctor say?

> MUGSY
> I have to tell you something.

> KAREN
> What? What is it?

> MUGSY
> Karen.

> KAREN
> What? You're scaring me, Mugsy.

MUGSY
(*slowly, breaking up each syllable*)
I am a gay homosexual.

Karen just stares at him for second, then makes a face.

KAREN
Mugsy, don't scare me. I hate it when you try an' scare me
like that.

She smacks him with the towel.

MUGSY
I'm not playing. I'm serious about it.

Mugsy watches her face for some kind of expression.

(*softly*)
I don't want to be around any women any more.

KAREN
What are you talkin' about, Mugsy?

MUGSY
I just don't want to be around any women any more.

KAREN
You don't want to be around women?

MUGSY
You remember last night?

KAREN
Yeah.

MUGSY
When we watched that movie?

KAREN
Yes, I do.

MUGSY
Well, I'll tell you. Something happened to me. I was
reborn.

Karen looks at him with a very concerned face.

When I saw that movie last night, I realized that I was a
gay. It was like when I was a child and people made fun of
me and then I just discovered Christ. Same as you did,
Karen. Only now I've been reborn as a gay.

> KAREN
>
> That doesn't make one bit of sense.

> MUGSY
>
> I don't expect you to think it does. All I know is it's natu-
> ral for me, it's the natural way I feel.

> KAREN
>
> There is no way that a person can just watch a movie and
> decide to turn gay. That doesn't make any sense and you
> know it doesn't, Mugsy.

> MUGSY
>
> All I know is it makes sense for me. I am very serious.

> KAREN
>
> You are?

> MUGSY
>
> I am serious, Karen.

> KAREN
>
> You're tellin' me you're gay?

Mugsy nods his head.

> MUGSY
> (*stern*)
>
> Yes. I even know my type.

> KAREN
>
> Shut up.

> MUGSY
>
> I like men who are muscular but not too muscular. And I
> like long hair.

A long pause as the two of them stare at each other.

Karen folds her arms and looks at the ground.

INT. SHOPPING MALL — DAY

Mugsy is slowly walking through the crowded mall. He is wearing an old Iron Maiden T-shirt with small holes on one of the shoulders.

People of all ages are coming out of the stores.

Mugsy is looking around.

INT. SHOPPING MALL BATHROOM — DAY

Mugsy walks in.

All the urinals are full so Mugsy waits for a moment on line.

As soon as one of the urinals is open Mugsy walks up.

He unzips his pants.

He glances over at a tall black man peeing beside him.

He looks over to the other side.

He looks down at his own pecker, then he nonchalantly peeks over at the tall black man's bottom private.

He does this in a slightly hurried disfranchised manner.

The tall black man flushes and walks away.

Another man steps up to the urinal.

Mugsy just stands there for a while, looking around, pretending to pee, hoping to catch a glimpse of someone's penis.

INT. MUGSY AND KAREN'S BATHROOM — DAY

Karen is standing up in front of the sink.

She is talking to herself as she looks in the mirror.

She is wearing a baggy teal terry-cloth bathrobe. Her eyes look a bit red and swollen from crying.

KAREN

Lord, lord, lord, lord, lord, lord, lord, lord, lord, lord, lord, lord.

She shakes her head.

What have you done to me? I ask you. What have you done to me? All along I try to be good. You throw so many hardships in my path. You make everything so difficult. You keep testing me. You do. Did you know that?

She begins to nod her head up and down.

(*almost in tears, her lips quivering*)
You do, lord. Yes you do. Oh yes you do. Yes you do, lord. I just want to be righteous. I don't want to be hurt any more. I'm through with that. No more pain. Pain pain go away, please come back another day.

She blows her nose with some toilet paper.

Lordy, lordy, lordy.

She looks over and sees Mugsy's red hat with his name embroidered on the front. It's resting on the top of the toilet.

She picks it up and runs out of the bathroom.

EXT. MUGSY AND KAREN'S BACK YARD — DAY

Karen comes running out the back door.

She is holding Mugsy's red cap in one hand and a bottle of lighter fluid in the other.

She looks possessed as she trots across the lawn in her bare feet.

The sound of wind blowing is very loud. It should sound as if it were blowing directly into a microphone or a storm were on its way. The sound of her feet in the wet grass is also heard.

The lawn is completely sparse except for one small solitary tree with no leaves.

Karen stops in front of the tree.

She places Mugsy's red hat on one of the tree branches so that it dangles like a Christmas ornament.

She opens the tin can of lighter fluid and begins to sloppily spray it all over the hat and branch. A little bit falls onto the sleeve of her bathrobe.

The sound of a dog barking is coming from next door.

She strikes a match and sets her husband's hat on fire.

She takes a few steps back and watches the hat burn.

She puts her hands on her hips. She seems a bit out of breath.

The fire quickly spreads to the branch and begins to burn the tree as the flames grow higher.

She walks up to the tree and swats at the branch.

KAREN

Damn it!

The fire catches hold of Karen's sleeve, but she doesn't notice it at first.

She is hastily trying to break the branch off.

The fire takes hold of the other branches and begins to burn.

Karen looks at her sleeve and screams.

She starts swatting her sleeve.

The fire on her sleeve quickly spreads to her back. She starts jumping up and down and swatting herself.

She is screaming at the top of her voice.

The fire lights up her entire body.

It takes hold of her white hair.

She runs around for a moment and then falls to her knees.

The dog next door is barking hysterically.

The entire tree is engulfed in flames.

Karen is on the ground, burning.

INT. HOSPITAL HALLWAY – BURN UNIT – DAY

Mugsy is standing in front of a door.

Two doctors in white robes are talking to him. He has his head down. Every so often he nods. He is holding a brown paper bag in one hand.

One of the doctors opens the door.

Mugsy walks in.

EXT. MUGSY AND KAREN'S BACK YARD – DAY

The tree is burnt to a crisp.

All that's left is a charred black trunk.

The grass surrounding the area is black and burnt.

A dog barks.

INT. HOSPITAL ROOM – DAY

Mugsy walks in with a blank expression on his face.

He is wearing a suit and tie, and his hair is parted neatly down the center.

The room is completely white and sterile.

Karen is lying on her stomach in a special bed that suspends her almost like a hammock. She is totally covered in white gauze bandages. The only parts of her body that are visible are her crystal clear eyes and her bare feet with the red toenail polish neatly intact. She is hooked up to an electronic support system. A long full-body mirror is in place below her.

Mugsy pulls a chair up and sits down beside her.

He looks at the reflection of her eyes in the mirror.

MUGSY

(with a lot of feeling, like he's talking to a small child)
Hi, Karen. How you doin', huh? You OK in there? How
do you feel? Can you breathe all right? It still hurts?

He opens up the paper bag and looks inside.

You know it's gonna be Easter in a few days. You like
Easter, don't ya?

He pulls out a beautiful pink Easter egg with glitter and decorations.

I made these myself.

He places the egg on the side of her bed.

*He has several eggs in the bag, all of them beautifully decorated in
an assortment of rainbow colors.*

One after the other he lines them up in a row on her bed.

It took me a really long time to make them. I think they're
beautiful. Don't you, Karen? I remember how you love
Easter.

He sticks his face close to her ear.

Are the drugs starting to numb the sores a bit? It still
hurts?

He looks at her eyes for some sign of life, but they are totally blank.

*He stands up and scoots the chair over to the wall. He walks over
and turns the television on.*

*He flips through the channels until a cartoon comes on, then he
mutes the volume.*

*He sits back down in the chair and looks at Karen lying there completely motionless with an ornate collection of Easter eggs next to
her.*

He crosses his legs and itches his scalp.

*He looks down at the watch on his wrist and then in one abrupt
motion begins to hold his breath.*

His cheeks pop out.

We watch him do this until his face turns a sickly color purple.

After about a minute and a half he looks down at his watch and exhales.

He gets a huge smile on his face.

He uncrosses his legs.

Karen, I broke the record!!

He takes a deep breath.

The color in his face returns to its natural albino white.

The screen goes to black.

★

The same circus music from the opening credits begins to play. After about ten seconds the music shuts off.

We hear the voice of Marion, a soft-spoken sixteen-year-old girl. She speaks slowly and slightly broken.

> MARION (V.O.)
> Then there was the blind girl who went to a nudist colony. It was a touching sight.

INT. BATHROOM — DAY

Marion is sitting still on top of the toilet seat. She is staring straight ahead.

She is blind. She is young and simple looking. Her hair is sandy blonde and knotted. Her skin is fair and there are freckles on her face. She is wearing flowery panties, a dull yellow tank top, and white tube socks pulled up all the way.

The word 'HERPES' appears in the top left-hand corner of the screen.

The bathroom is small and plain. The toilet is almost touching the sink. There is a pack of cigarettes and a lighter sitting on the edge of the sink.

Marion lets out a humongous yawn.

She feels around the edge of the sink for the cigarettes.

She lights up and then sets the pack on her thigh.

She blows the smoke out in a long steady stream.

CUT TO:

Marion is standing up in front of the sink.

She takes out a small wash cloth and begins to scrub vigorously under her arms.

CUT TO:

Marion brushing her teeth with purple toothpaste. Her teeth are a bit crooked. She gets a little toothpaste on her cheek and then quickly wipes it off with the back of her hand.

She spits into the sink.

INT. MARION'S ROOM — DAY

Marion opens the door and walks in.

Her room is neat and almost completely bare. It looks like no one lives in it, no personal touches at all except for a large yellow parrot in a cage that is hanging from the ceiling. The bed is made very neat.

As Marion walks toward her closet we hear the parrot scream out in an extremely annoying squeal.

> BOBO THE PARROT
> (*very quickly*)
> Hello, Marion. Where you been? Where you been?

> MARION
> I was in the bathroom, Bobo.

Marion slides open her closet door.

> BOBO THE PARROT
> Hello, Marion. Where you been? Where you been?

Marion walks across her room and feels for the cage.

Where you been? Where you been?

Marion sticks her face up to the cage.

MARION
I was in the bathroom, Bobo. Shhhh!

The parrot starts jumping around in its cage. Marion's older sister Cordelia walks in the room.

CORDELIA
Stop talking to birds, Marion.

Marion nervously turns around and looks toward Cordelia.

Cordelia is around eighteen years old. She is skinny and attractive in an unusual way. Her features are a bit cold and her demeanor is mysterious, and she has piercing blue eyes. Her hair is shoulder length and straight down. She is wearing blue jeans and a tight Rod Stewart T-shirt.

Did you pick out what you're gonna wear?

MARION
Not yet.

Cordelia starts flipping through her sister's closet.

Marion walks over.

I was considering wearing my new skirt with just a sweater or some kind of blouse or something.

CORDELIA
What new skirt?

Marion feels through her clothes until she touches her skirt, then she pulls it out half way.

That's not new.

MARION
It's new.

CORDELIA

I can remember you've been wearing that for a while.

MARION

I bought it three weeks ago.

CORDELIA

It seems like you always wear it.

Marion pushes it back.

Cordelia starts flipping through her sister's clothes like she's in a hurry.

She stops when she gets to a silver leotard. She takes it out and puts it in front of Marion.

What about the leotard?

Marion grabs the crotch of the leotard and squeezes it with her fingers.

You should just wear this. Put some pants on underneath and it'll look cool. Put on your dark denim jeans.

MARION

You think?

Cordelia sticks the leotard up against Marion's body.

CORDELIA

Yeah, that's a pretty outfit.

Marion walks over to her bed and sits down with the leotard on her lap.

Cordelia puts her hands on her sides.

Maybe you could put a pin on it or something to spruce it up.

MARION

Yeah.

Cordelia pulls some blue jeans from out of her sister's dresser drawer and tosses them onto the bed.

*She looks at Marion sitting still on the bed in her panties. She has a
blank expression on her face.*

CORDELIA

You're getting a little pouch on your belly.

The parrot screams out two high-pitched yelps in a row.

Cordelia walks over and squeezes Marion's stomach.

Marion swats her hand away.

MARION

Don't.

Cordelia puts her hand back on Marion's stomach.

Don't!

*Cordelia looks at Marion's face. Marion's eyes are wide open. Her
blindness causes her head to shift slightly back and forth.*

Cordelia stares for a moment then touches Marion's face.

CORDELIA

You should put on some make-up.

MARION

Yeah.

CORDELIA

Some lipstick at least.

MARION
(nodding her head 'yes')

I was gonna.

Cordelia stands up and itches her nose, then walks out of the room.

*Marion, still sitting on her bed in her panties, picks up the silver leo-
tard and swings it back and forth in front of her.*

INT. KITCHEN – DAY

*The kitchen is quaint and orderly. There is a small dishwasher and a
yellow refrigerator next to some open windows. An electric coffee-*

maker is half-way full on the counter next to the sink.

Marion opens the refrigerator and pulls out a carton of milk. She is wearing an extremely thick gloss of red lipstick.

She sets the milk on the table.

She opens a little pantry and pulls out a box of candy-coated cereal.

It is apparent by the way she moves around the kitchen that she is familiar with the layout.

She sits down at the table and begins to eat.

When a little bit of milk falls down the side of her mouth she takes a paper towel and gently wipes it away.

She continues to eat, making loud crunching sounds.

EXT. BUS STOP — DAY

Marion and Cordelia are sitting down next to two middle-aged black women. Both women are talking to each other with large bags of groceries in their laps.

Marion and Cordelia are scrunched together smoking cigarettes.

Marion is wearing her leotard and pants with an orange scarf tied tightly around her neck.

The wind is blowing their hair.

INT. BUS — DAY

The bus is fairly crowded. All the seats are taken and there are a few people standing up in the aisle.

Marion and Cordelia are sitting next to each other in the back of the bus.

Toward the middle of the bus is a seventeen-year-old boy with long shaggy brown hair. He is sitting down listening to his headphones.

Cordelia begins to stare at him.

The boy is looking straight ahead. Occasionally he taps his legs like

*he's playing the drums. His shoelaces are untied and there is a hole
in the armpit of his sweater.*

                              MARION
       Cordelia.

                              CORDELIA
       What?

                              MARION
                            (*quietly*)
       Are you looking at a boy?

                              CORDELIA
       Yeah.

The bus goes over a big bump.

                              MARION
       Is he cute?

                              CORDELIA
       He's very cute.

                              MARION
       What does he look like?

                              CORDELIA
       I don't know.

Marion looks toward the floor.

Cordelia continues to stare.

                              MARION
       Does he have dark hair?

                              CORDELIA
       Aha.

                              MARION
       What do his eyes look like?

                              CORDELIA
       Shh.

MARION

Are his eyes brown?

CORDELIA

I can't see his eyes. But he's got long hair.

MARION

Is that the kind of boy you like?

CORDELIA

What kind of boy?

MARION

Like him.

CORDELIA

I don't know. There's not like one type or anything.
Except I prefer tall and skinny types best.

MARION

Is he your type?

CORDELIA

He could be, I don't know. I'd have to talk to him first.

MARION

Why don't you?

CORDELIA

Shut up.

MARION

If he's your type, you should.

CORDELIA

I didn't say he's my type.

MARION

But he could be.

Cordelia says nothing.

Does he have a moustache?

CORDELIA

No, I hate moustaches.

MARION

Are you gonna talk to him?

CORDELIA

No, I don't have anything to say to him.

MARION

Well, what if he's your type?

Cordelia opens a stick of gum and begins to chew.

You can't describe his features any better to me?

CORDELIA

No I can't, Marion. I wish you'd shut up.

The bus stops.

The boy gets off without ever noticing the girls.

He just got off.

MARION

I guess you missed your chance.

They ride in silence for a bit.

The road is bumpy.

Are there any other cute boys on the bus?

CORDELIA

No.

They continue to ride.

EXT. SIDEWALK — DAY

Marion and Cordelia are walking down the sidewalk. Marion is holding Cordelia's wrist tightly and they are walking at a fairly slow pace.

Cars are zooming by.

Birds are chirping loudly.

INT. BALLET STUDIO — WAITING ROOM — DAY

Marion and Cordelia enter the waiting room of a medium-sized ballet studio.

The sound of someone playing the piano is heard. Also we can hear a woman yelling out instructions.

Middle-aged mothers are sitting around talking to each other.

Two five-year-old boys are playing with building blocks in the middle of the floor.

As Marion and Cordelia make their way through, some of the women look up and stare.

Marion looks a bit nervous.

Cordelia walks Marion over toward a big glass window that looks directly into the ballet studio.

The class is full with around thirty young girls all dressed up in pink tights and leg warmers.

There is a huge mirror that circles one half of the entire studio.

A short and skinny female dance instructor is prancing around the center of the floor shouting out instructions. Her hair is tied up in a bun. As she walks, she slides her feet gracefully on the scraped wooden floor.

A bald man in a tweed jacket is playing the piano. Both sisters are looking out the window.

MARION

It sounds nice in there.

The young ballerinas begin to dance around.

One by one they twirl in front of the window and then exit through the door.

The dance instructor begins clapping her hands. She has a serious look on her face.

DANCE INSTRUCTOR
Good class! Good class! See you next week!

The dance instructor pats one of the little girls on the head and then smiles.

Come early next week for stretch class!

Marion and Cordelia are watching.

The dance instructor walks over and begins talking to the man at the piano.

A stream of young ballerinas parade past Marion and Cordelia and run to their mothers.

A few of the little girls bump into the side of Marion's leg as they run through the door.

Marion scoots over against the wall.

The noise is loud with all the girls laughing and screaming.

The dance instructor walks out of the studio into the waiting room. She is rubbing the back of her neck with a white towel.

CORDELIA
(*whispering to Marion*)
Here comes the teacher.

As the dance instructor walks into the room, she stops and talks to one of the mothers.

Cordelia takes Marion by the wrist and walks over. The dance instructor says goodbye to the women and then turns around.

Are you the head instructor here?

DANCE INSTRUCTOR
Yes, I am.

CORDELIA
Um, my name is Cordelia and this is my sister Marion.

Marion smiles nervously and looks past the dance instructor's head.

The dance instructor looks down at Cordelia holding her sister's wrist.

> DANCE INSTRUCTOR

Hi.

> CORDELIA

We just wanted to get some information about signing up to take a dance class.

> DANCE INSTRUCTOR

OK, why don't you come with me to my office.

The dance instructor turns her back and walks quickly down a narrow hallway.

Some of the little ballerinas are still running around.

Cordelia and Marion follow.

INT. DANCE INSTRUCTOR'S OFFICE – DAY

The office is small and cluttered with papers and boxes. The room is completely square with no windows, and the wall is made of cheap wood paneling. A TV set and VCR is sitting on a black metal stand with piles of video cassettes stacked underneath. There are a few ballet posters on the wall. There is a large framed poster directly behind the desk. It's a picture of two worn-out ballet shoes with big holes in them. Underneath the picture the caption reads: 'SOME GIRLS LOVE TO DANCE, WHILE OTHERS DANCE TO LOVE.'

The dance instructor waits for the girls to enter the room, then she shuts the door and sits down behind her desk.

Cordelia guides Marion to one of the seats in front of the desk.

The dance instructor watches with a curious look on her face.

Cordelia remains standing.

> DANCE INSTRUCTOR

So, what would you like to know?

CORDELIA

Well, we were referred here, actually one of my friends referred us here.

DANCE INSTRUCTOR

Who?

CORDELIA

Rita Levy.

DANCE INSTRUCTOR

Sure, I know Rita. She doesn't dance here any more. She used to take tap and modern here.

Cordelia nods her head 'yes.'

Marion is looking at the floor.

Well, what do you want to sign up for?

CORDELIA

Well, it's not for me actually. I don't want to sign up. It's for Marion.

MARION

Yeah, I would like to dance if there is any more room in your classes.

The dance instructor looks at Marion.

DANCE INSTRUCTOR
(*a bit confused*)

OK.

CORDELIA

My sister is blind but she would like to take a ballet class.

DANCE INSTRUCTOR

You want to take a ballet class?

MARION

Yes, I would love it.

DANCE INSTRUCTOR

Uhu, ooh, the thing is that I'm not sure.

Marion looks up in the general direction of the dance instructor's face.

I'm not sure how I could do it. I'm uncertain of, well, you know . . .
                    (*nervous laughter*)
. . . of how to teach you properly because I've never done it before.

CORDELIA
She's just interested in the most intermediate class possible.

MARION
(*smiling*)
Yeah, I don't want to take anything too hard or advanced. I'd just want to take a class for beginners . . .

DANCE INSTRUCTOR
Right.

MARION
'Cause I've never really danced before.

DANCE INSTRUCTOR
Well, I would love to teach you, I just don't know if I could do a really good job or not.

CORDELIA
You wouldn't have to really teach her, I mean, she could just listen and follow along and just, you know, do her own thing.

DANCE INSTRUCTOR
Right, no, I understand, it's just that that's not the way I like to teach.
                    (*staring at Marion*)
If I did teach you ballet I would really try and teach you ballet and spend time on it with you.

MARION
Yeah.

DANCE INSTRUCTOR
Unfortunately, because it's just me and one other instructor here, it makes it really hard to set aside that kind of time that it would take.

She looks up at Cordelia.

You see what I'm saying?

MARION
(*quietly*)
Yeah.

Marion coughs into her hand.

CORDELIA
Yeah, but I know her, and it wouldn't be hard. She wouldn't even say anything, she just wants to be able to do some simple steps.

MARION
Yeah, I don't even care about learning pirouettes.

The dance instructor smiles and then pops one of her knuckles back.

DANCE INSTRUCTOR
Well, you know what I can do? I can take your number down and check into it for you. I can make a few phone calls. Maybe there's a special class somewhere. I'm sure there's gotta be one somewhere around town.

All three sit in silence for a bit.

MARION
No, it's OK.

She grabs the side of the chair and stands up.

Thank you anyway.

The dance instructor stands up.

DANCE INSTRUCTOR
Are you sure? It really wouldn't be a problem for me to find out for you.

CORDELIA
(*cold*)

No, it's OK.

Cordelia takes Marion by the hand and walks toward the door.

Marion is still smiling.

MARION

What about any slippers?

The dance instructor walks over toward the door.

DANCE INSTRUCTOR

Slippers?

MARION

Yeah, dance slippers. Do you sell them here?

DANCE INSTRUCTOR

Yeah, we sell ballet shoes. You want a pair? What size are you?

MARION

Size seven.

DANCE INSTRUCTOR

We have black and pink.

MARION
(*smiling*)

I'd prefer pink please.

Cordelia walks quietly with Marion out of the dance instructor's office.

INT. BALLET STUDIO – WAITING ROOM – DAY

Marion and Cordelia are standing still.

A group of new ballet girls are running around, talking to each other and doing stretches on the floor. These girls are around the same age as Marion.

The dance instructor comes back holding a box of shoes.

Marion digs into her pocket and pulls out a small red wallet.

She takes some cash out and then hands it to the dance instructor.

The dance instructor smiles and takes the money, then hands the box of slippers over to Marion.

INT. ICE-CREAM SHOP – DAY

Marion and Cordelia are standing in the middle of the store licking large multicolored ice-cream cones.

A muzak version of the Beatles song 'Eleanor Rigby' is playing softly in the background.

An obese black man is mopping the floor.

EXT. SIDEWALK – DAY

Cordelia is holding Marion's arm as they cross the street at a red light.

The birds are chirping and the wind is blowing.

INT. BOWLING ALLEY – DAY

Cordelia and Marion enter a nice-sized bowling alley.

The sound of pins dropping is heard. The place is about half-way full, people are walking around, and a young woman with a feathered hair-do and long silver earrings is behind the counter passing out shoes and signing people up. Metal lockers line the entire back wall.

Near the entrance, they pass by a small games room with teenagers playing ping-pong and pool.

As they make their way through, Cordelia sees a group of about seven of her friends hanging around the last lane by the wall.

CORDELIA

There they are.

Cordelia looks happy.

She holds Marion's wrist and quickly guides her over.

Cordelia's friends all look about the same age, except for the boy taking score, who looks about thirty. The group is half boys and half girls. They all look pretty clean-cut and average. A few of the boys are wearing dirty white baseball caps.

Two of the girls notice Cordelia walking over and they jump up.

Girl 1 runs up and gives Cordelia a huge hug. She has long frizzy blonde hair and a cross necklace.

CORDELIA

Hi!!

GIRL 1

Cordelia! How are you, baby!?

Cordelia gives her a kiss on the cheek.

Hey, Marion.

MARION

Hi, how are you?

A tall white kid with braces bowls a gutter ball.

All of his friends start to clap.

He pounds his hands together and does a goofy little dance.

Cordelia and Marion walk over to the group.

All the girls jump up and hug Cordelia.

Girl 2, who is wearing really short yellow shorts, puts her hand on the top of Marion's head and rubs it around.

GIRL 2

Hi there.

MARION

Hi, how are you doin'?

GIRL 2

Fine, fine.

They are all drinking beer out of white styrofoam cups. An almost empty pitcher of beer is resting on the back table.

All the boys say hello to Cordelia.

Boy 1 kisses her on the cheek. He's wearing a small earring and a backwards baseball cap.

Marion finds her way to an empty seat behind the table.

Cordelia looks over at Marion and then begins to socialize with the group.

> BOY 1

You gonna bowl?

> CORDELIA

I don't know. Should I?

> BOY 1

Yeah, go get some shoes.

> CORDELIA

Bowling shoes?

> BOY 1
> (*pointing*)

Yeah, right over there.

> CORDELIA

All right.

Cordelia runs over to get some shoes with Girl 1 and Girl 2.

Marion is sitting quietly in the back.

Boy 2 bowls a really fast one, but only knocks over two pins.

> BOY 1

You suck!! You suck!!

Boy 2 flips him a bird.

> BOY 2

Fuck off.

The young woman with the feathered hair-do hands Cordelia a pair of bowling shoes.

Boy 3 sits down one seat away from Marion. He is the dorkiest of the bunch, with acid-washed jeans and bad acne.

He pulls out a cigarette and begins to smoke. He's watching his friends bowl.

Marion smiles and looks in his general direction.

MARION
Do you have another cigarette by any chance?

BOY 3
Sure.

He hands her one, but it takes her a second to grab it out of his hand.

She sticks it in her mouth.

He looks at her for a second then reaches deep into his back pant pocket.

Need a light?

MARION
Yeah.

She sticks her head forward.

He flicks open a metal lighter and lights her cigarette. Her head is shaking a little bit.

Cordelia is at the other end of the bowling alley trying to pick out a ball with her two friends.

CORDELIA
(*holding a ball in one hand*)
It's too heavy.

GIRL 1
They're all too heavy.

Girl 2 picks up a ball with both her hands.

GIRL 2

Here, try this one.

Marion is blowing smoke out of her nose.

Boy 3 is looking at her.

BOY 3

You want some beer?

MARION

Sure I do.

She smiles and then crosses her legs.

He leans over and pours her a cup.

BOY 3

Here.

He hands it to her.

MARION

Thanks.

She immediately starts drinking it.

BOY 3

You're Cordelia's sister?

MARION

Yeah, my name is Marion.

BOY 3

Are you gonna bowl?

MARION
(*smiling*)

I don't think so, because I'm blind.

Boy 1 runs up and grabs Boy 3 on the shoulder.

BOY 1

It's your go, man.

BOY 3

OK.

Boy 3 jumps up and walks away.

Marion turns her head as he walks away. She looks disappointed.

Cordelia returns with her ball and shoes.

She sits down and begins to talk and laugh with the rest of her friends.

Marion drinks the rest of her beer in one long gulp.

Boy 3 throws his ball with much grace and ease. He knocks all but one pin down.

Marion stands up and feels her way to the back of the room.

No one notices her.

When she gets to where the lockers are, she sticks her hand out and begins to walk forward using the lockers as a guide.

Her hand smacking against the locks makes a loud noise.

She walks slowly down the back of the bowling alley until she reaches the girls' bathroom at the opposite end.

She feels for the door and then enters.

INT. BOWLING ALLEY — REST ROOM — DAY

Marion enters the large bathroom.

It is extremely bright with fluorescent lights, the kind of light that makes your skin look yellow and every pore and crease on your face becomes incredibly visible. There are two stalls in the corner and a big sink with a dirty mirror on the other side.

No one else is in the bathroom.

Marion feels her way to the stall nearest to the end.

She walks inside and locks the door behind her.

From underneath the stall we can see her pants bunched up around her shoes.

The sound of her peeing is heard.

Then the sound of a loud toilet bowl flushing is heard.

We can see the bottom of her pants come up.

Marion opens the stall door and walks out.

She feels her way to the dirty sinks. Brown paper towels are tossed around the edges.

She opens the faucet and a powerful stream of water shoots out.

She washes her hands and neck.

She shuts the water off.

She feels around for some towels and then dries herself.

She sticks her hand in her front pant pocket and pulls out a few dollar bills and a small vial of lipstick.

She sets the lipstick on the sink, then shoves the money back into her pocket.

The bathroom door opens and the young lady with the feathered hair from behind the counter walks in. She is carrying a large fake leather handbag. Her earrings are so long that they smack against the sides of her chin. She walks up to the sink, next to Marion, and pulls out a hair brush.

She begins brushing her hair.

Marion pauses for a moment then starts applying her lipstick.

The young lady looks over at Marion.

She continues to brush her hair, then she stops and puts her hair brush down.

YOUNG LADY

Dear, that's not how you do it.

Marion looks a bit startled.

MARION

Excuse me?

YOUNG LADY

You don't put on lipstick like that.

MARION

Yeah?

YOUNG LADY

The way you're doing it makes it spread way too thick.

MARION

Actually I was goofing around with it. I don't usually wear it so much.

YOUNG LADY

You want me to show you how to do it?

MARION

Show me?

YOUNG LADY

Yeah. Put it on proper?

MARION

I guess so.

YOUNG LADY

Lemme see it.

The young lady grabs the lipstick out of Marion's hand.

Marion coughs into her hand.

First you have to take it off.

The young lady takes a paper towel and wets it, then she wipes Marion's lips clean.

She throws the towel onto the counter.

Now pucker your lips up.

Marion puckers her lips.

Good.

The young lady slowly spreads the lipstick evenly onto Marion's lips.

That's all, like that.

MARION

Yeah.

YOUNG LADY

Just like that.

The young lady picks up another paper towel.

Now open your mouth up a tad.

The young lady sticks the paper towel between Marion's lips.

Now pat down with your lips.

Marion pats her lips down.

Pat down again.

Marion pats down again.

The young lady tosses the paper towel into the sink.

MARION

How does it look?

YOUNG LADY

I think it looks about perfect.

Marion smiles.

You have some crooked teeth there, don't you?

MARION

I never had any braces.

The young lady grabs her pocket book and begins to walk out of the bathroom.

Marion turns around.

Do you think I could touch your face?

The young lady stops short of the door.

> YOUNG LADY
> (*smiling*)

Touch my face?

> MARION

So I can feel your features.

> YOUNG LADY

My features?

> MARION

Yeah, can I feel your features?

The young lady walks over and grabs Marion's hand.

She takes her hand and softly places it on the top of her forehead.

Both girls look serious.

Marion very slowly slides the palm of her hand over the young lady's face.

When she gets to the lips, she stops and feels them very closely.

She begins to lightly pinch the corner of the young lady's upper lip.

What's that?

> YOUNG LADY

That little bump?

> MARION

Yeah.

> YOUNG LADY

It's a herpes.

> MARION

Does it hurt?

> YOUNG LADY

Not really.

Marion drops her hand to her side.

INT. BOWLING ALLEY — DAY

Cordelia throws the ball down and rolls a perfect strike.

She coolly turns around and winks at one of the boys.

Girl 1 runs up and claps her hand.

                              CORDELIA
  Whooo!

EXT. SIDEWALK — STREET — EVENING

The sun is going down. A purplish glow casts itself as Marion and Cordelia cross the street.

A few young boys ride their bicycles past.

Marion is holding Cordelia's shoulder with one hand and a box of ballet slippers in the other.

They come before a curb.

                              CORDELIA
  Step up.

They walk up onto the sidewalk.

INT./EXT. BUS — EVENING

The bus is almost empty.

Marion and Cordelia are sitting quietly in the very front.

Cordelia is watching the bus driver steer.

Marion is staring straight forward.

As the bus sways, the girls bump around in perfect unison.

INT. HOUSE — KITCHEN — DAY

The girls open the front door to their house and walk into the kitchen.

Cordelia flips the light on.

CORDELIA
(*screaming*)
Mom! Mom! Is anyone home?

There is no answer.

There's no one home.

Marion walks a few feet.

Both girls seem a little bit tired.

MARION
Are you gonna make some food?

CORDELIA
I guess so.

MARION
What are you gonna cook?

CORDELIA
What do you feel like?

MARION
Spaghetti.

CORDELIA
You want spaghetti?

MARION
Yeah.

CORDELIA
OK.

Cordelia tosses the house keys onto the kitchen counter.

MARION
Do you want me to help you?

CORDELIA
No, it's OK. I can make spaghetti real quick.

Marion walks out of the room.

INT. STAIRWAY — EVENING

Marion walks out of the kitchen and climbs up a flight of carpeted stairs.

She grabs onto the wooden rail and makes her way up.

INT. BATHROOM — DAY

Marion opens the light.

She shuts the door behind her.

She opens the cabinet underneath the sink and pulls out a crumpled pack of cigarettes and a small plastic see-through green lighter.

She sits down on the top of the toilet seat.

She begins to smoke.

After a few deep puffs, Cordelia opens the door and walks in.

She shuts the door behind her.

She sits down on the edge of the bathtub and sweeps her hair back in one grand motion.

                    CORDELIA
     You have an extra one?

Marion hands her a cigarette and the lighter.

The two girls puff.

Cordelia picks something off the tip of her tongue.

Marion is facing straight ahead.

Cordelia looks at Marion smoking and then begins to grin.

     Tired?

                    MARION
     A little bit.

> CORDELIA

What time did you wake up this morning?

> MARION

Early.

> CORDELIA

Me too.

Cordelia takes one last quick puff, then sticks the butt of her cigarette under the faucet.

She tosses it into the trash.

She stands up and walks toward the door.

Dinner will be done soon.

> MARION
> (*still smoking*)

All right.

Cordelia walks out of the bathroom.

INT. MARION'S BEDROOM — EVENING

Marion walks in and turns on the light.

She locks the door behind her.

She is holding her box under one arm.

Bobo the parrot starts jumping around its cage.

The parrot seems extremely excited that Marion has returned.

Marion walks over and sets the box down on her bed.

> BOBO THE PARROT

Hello, Marion. Where you been? Where you been?

> MARION

I went out, Bobo. Is that OK with you?

Bobo starts going crazy.

Marion walks over to the cage and sticks the front of her nose through one of the tiny bars.

Bobo the parrot flutters its wings and jumps onto her nose and then jumps back off.

BOBO THE PARROT

Hello, Marion. Where you been? Where you been?

MARION

I went out, Bobo.

Marion does a quick high-pitched whistle.

Bobo the parrot continues to jump around with excitement.

Marion pulls her nose from out of the cage and then walks back to her bed.

She sits down next to the box on her bed.

She pulls her pants off her legs so that the only thing she is wearing is her silver leotard and her orange scarf.

She opens the box up and takes out two pink leather ballet slippers, size seven.

She sticks them up to her nose and smells them.

She holds them for a second then she places them on her feet.

They make her feet look very dainty.

She points her toes straight out.

Bobo the parrot whistles the first few bars from 'Dixie.'

Marion stands up and raises her arms like a ballerina.

She begins to dance.

It is absolutely silent except for the sound of Bobo the parrot.

Marion is jumping around and swinging her arms through the air.

She does a clumsy little spin on one leg and then smiles.

She leaps around her room, never bumping into anything.

BOBO THE PARROT

Marion is a good dancer! Marion is a good dancer!

Marion stops and does a curtsy a few feet from the parrot's cage.

Hello, Marion. Where you been? Where you been?

Marion parts her arms to the side and bows her head.

CUT TO BLACK.

Gummo

Gummo: Nick Sutton as Tummler, Jacob Reynolds as Solomon.

CAST AND CREW

MAIN CAST

BUNNY BOY	Jacob Sewell
TUMMLER	Nick Sutton
SOLOMON	Jacob Reynolds
DARBY	Darby Dougherty
DOT	Chloë Sevigny
HELEN	Carisa Glucksman
HUNTZ	Wendall Carr
EDDIE	Charles Matthew Coatney
BOY ON COUCH	Harmony Korine
MIDGET	Bryant L. Crenshaw
JARROD	Daniel Martin
EARL	Nathan Rutherford
COLE	Max Perlich
CASSIDEY	Bernadette Resna
SOLOMON'S MOM	Linda Manz
CHAIR WRESTLER	Mark Gonzales
TERRY	Jeffery Baker

MAIN CREW

Directed by	Harmony Korine
Written by	Harmony Korine
Produced by	Cary Woods
Co-producers	Robin O'Hara
	Scott Macauley
Executive producers	Stephen Chin
	Ruth Vitale
Cinematography by	Jean-Yves Escoffier
Film Editing by	Christopher Tellefsen
Casting by	Lyn Richmond
Production Design by	David Doernberg
Costume Design by	Chloë Sevigny

The screen starts out completely black. We hear someone struggling to breathe, mixed with the sound of heavy wind.

EXT. XENIA, OHIO – DAY

This is a movie that takes place in Xenia, Ohio.

STOCK FOOTAGE – *Super 8 newsreel of the famous tornado that hit the small town of Xenia in the early 1970s. This is perhaps the worst tornado in US history.*

The footage is grainy and in color, everything is blown out and frantic looking. It should look similar to the stuff you watched in your junior high-school science class on the lessons of natural disasters.

Houses are being smashed to pieces.

People are running around in a state of frenzy.

Trees are flying down dirty roads.

Children are crying.

The tornado smashes a supermarket into a million pieces.

Families are huddled together in basements.

The entire town is destroyed and turned upside down.

We hear the faint sound of wind blowing. It is very light and haunting.

We hear the voice of Solomon, a fourteen-year-old boy with a high-pitched squeaky voice. It should sound as if it were recorded on a crummy tape recorder.

SOLOMON (V.O.)

Xenia, Ohio. Xenia, Ohio. A few years ago a tornado hit this place. It killed people left and right. Dogs died. Cats

died. Houses were split open and you could see necklaces
hanging from branches of trees. People's legs and neck
bones were stickin' out. Oliver found a leg on his roof. A
lot of people's fathers died and were killed by the great
tornado. I saw a girl fly through the sky and I looked up
her skirt. The school was smashed and some kids died.
My neighbor was killed in half. He used to ride dirt bikes
and his three-wheelers. They never found his head. I
always thought that was funny. People died in Xenia.
Before dad died he got a bad case of the diabetes.

INT. HOSPITAL HALLWAY — DAY

*Dad is in a wheelchair rolling himself down a shabby small-town
hospital hallway.*

*He is fat and has a cast on his left foot. He is wearing a hospital
robe and on his other foot a thick pink sock. He has a fluffy head of
white hair. He is missing all his front teeth.*

The walls are bare and ugly.

The hallway is empty as he pushes himself slowly through.

INT. HOSPITAL CAFETERIA — DAY

*The cafeteria is basic and plain. It looks like it has not been refur-
bished in many years.*

*There are a lot of people sitting around eating and talking. Dad is
sitting next to an old white guy in blackface and dressed in an old
gray suit and a red bow tie.*

*The black guy is holding a black ventriloquist's doll in his lap. The doll
has a big head and is wearing the exact same outfit as the black guy.*

Dad is eating a bowl of green Jell-O and a large piece of carrot cake.

The black guy is drinking a carton of milk.

They are sitting side by side, not looking at each other.

Dad eats his food as he speaks.

DAD

How long have you been a clown?

BLACK GUY

I'm a ventriloquist.

DAD

Oh, that's nice.

BLACK GUY

When I got a disease some people said that they were happy that I was gonna die because I wasn't funny any more. I told them that I was sorry but my mother used to idolize Al Jolson and I loved him very dearly myself.

Dad takes a huge bite of his cake and continues to talk.

DAD

I got diabetes.

BLACK GUY

Did it hurt?

DAD

Well, it was stiff and clotted. It felt like a ball of fire at the tip by the nail.

BLACK GUY

Did it hurt to take it off?

DAD

No, I was under anesthetic. I woke up and tried to move it.

BLACK GUY

Afterwards?

DAD

After the operation.

BLACK GUY

You thought it was still on?

DAD

Yeah. I cried when I looked at my foot. It looked fake. I

don't think my sandals are gonna fit right. My foot is
lighter. And when I stood up, my toes spread different.

The black guy laughs.

They spread all wider and uneven because there was no
middle toe to block it.

BLACK GUY

Ooooof.

DAD

My son Solomon gave me a toenail clipper as a joke. I saw
a documentary on Cambodians who set off land mines.
There was this one fourteen-year-old Cambodian boy
named Sink Lou Low. He blew his right leg off in a rice
paddy. They gave him a fake tin leg that went up to his
pelvis. And when he walked for the first time with his new
leg, there were people all along the sides of him. I imagine
some family and friends. They got up and started clapping. They were making jokes and laughing.

He picks up the doll and starts making it bop around on the table.

They started screaming, 'Sink Lou Low, Sink Lou Low.'
And I swear to you, he started dancing right there.

Dad laughs with the Jell-O in his mouth.

He was dancing to them, singing out his name. And on
the end of his tin leg was a rubber foot.

BLACK GUY

A rubber foot?

DAD

A rubber foot. It was a real rubber foot. It was beautiful.

Close-up of the doll dancing clumsily on the table top.

BLACK GUY (O.S.)

I wonder if I should get a rubber toe?

CUT TO THE TITLE:

'GUMMO' *is written in small neat white typewritten letters on an all-black background.*

In a high-pitched cartoon-like voice we hear someone singing, 'My sperm is the greatest sperm in the world.'

CUT TO:

Opening credits.

EXT. SUBURBAN STREET – DAY

The opening credits roll on top of an image of a skinny twelve-year-old boy wearing pink rabbit ears. He is riding a slender yellow skateboard down a hill. He is wearing Bermuda shorts, no shirt, and a pair of velcro sneakers. The word 'MAC' is tattooed on his middle fingers.

The song 'My Little Rooster' by Almeda Riddle accompanies the credits.

The credits end.

CUT TO BLACK.

The loud sound of someone gargling mouthwash.

EXT. SUBURBAN STREET – DAY

A large gray cat is being held tightly by the scruff of its neck.

It's wiggling around and sticking its legs straight out.

We watch the hand drop the cat into a big barrel of water.

The cat tries to crawl out of the bucket but it's too weak to manage.

We watch as the cat struggles and then eventually drowns in the barrel of water.

All the while, no sound is heard except for the magnified sound of gargling.

The cat floats dead in the bucket.

INT. CAR — NIGHT

The sound continues.

The car is parked on the side of the dirt road. It is completely dark except for the light on in the car.

Tummler is sitting in the passenger side of the small car. His head is tilted back and he is gargling mouthwash.

A twenty-two-year-old redhead girl with rosy cheeks and lots of freckles on her face is sitting in the driver's seat. She is wearing a yellow turtle-neck sweater.

She sticks a styrofoam cup in front of Tummler's face.

REDHEAD GIRL
Spit it out.

He swishes the mouthwash around in his cheeks and then spits it into the cup.

She places the cup inside the beverage holder next to the gear shift.

They begin kissing.

Tummler is around nineteen or twenty. He looks like a cross between Baby Huey and a classic Gothic inbred: part trash, part Bible. He has blond hair and very fair skin. He has a long forehead and a big mouth. He likes to smile an evil grin all the time. He has a small cross tattooed on his wrist. When he speaks his voice breaks at every interval. There is something very beautiful about him. He is wearing a dirty white T-shirt with his name scrawled across the front in black marker.

As Tummler and the redhead girl kiss, Tummler begins to feel her breasts.

She lets him for a second then pushes his hand away.

Don't, Tummler.

He moves his hand away for a moment and then places it back, this time inside the sweater.

He begins to feel her up.

She starts breathing heavy.

Tummler starts kissing her neck.

She looks as if she is getting very excited.

She is rubbing his arm back and forth.

After a while of this, Tummler abruptly stops kissing her and just looks strangely into her eyes.

His hand is just holding her breast underneath her sweater.

She slowly lifts her head up and looks at Tummler.

What is it?

TUMMLER
You have a lump in there.

He squeezes her breast.

She knocks his hand out of her shirt and begins feeling her own breast.

A frightened look crosses her face.

That's a big ol' lump.

The loud sound of bicycle wheels spinning.

EXT. SUBURBAN STREET — DAY

Close-up of moving bicycle wheel.

Tummler and Solomon, fourteen, are riding bicycles down the middle of a paved street.

Solomon looks like no other boy in the world. Everything about him is odd. He is tall and extremely skinny, skin and bones. His hair is black and greased down on his face. Dandruff is apparent. His shoulders are pinched and drawn to his neck. He is pale and doughy. He almost looks like a cartoon character. When you look at him, it's hard to believe that he's a real person.

The two of them are riding their bicycles down an empty street.

Rows of small houses surround both sides of the street.

Both boys have BB guns strapped to their backs.

Solomon is wearing tight army pants with big pockets and an orange YMCA T-shirt. He has on a pair of generic high-top sneakers. His bike is red and simple, one wheel is a mag and the other is spoked.

Tummler is wearing a pair of blue jeans with patches on them. There are little holes in his pants. He is wearing a blue flannel shirt with grease stains. He has a green backpack on. His sneakers are old running shoes with the soles worn down. His bike is more glamorous; it is painted silver and has stickers on it. There is a racing plate on the front of the handlebars with the number 17 on it. He is sitting on a long padded banana seat. There is a skull and crossbones flag attached to the back of the bike. It flaps noisily in the wind.

They're both silent as they ride sitting down.

As they ride down the street they are looking in all directions. It seems as if they are trying to find something.

We watch them ride silently in a straight line for about two blocks.

Tummler stands up and looks excited.

Solomon sees Tummler stand and immediately does the same thing.

TUMMLER

     I see one. It's a blacky. Straight up.

They begin to speed up.

As they speed up, Tummler rides his bike directly into frame.

The frame becomes a snapshot of a photograph. It is followed by fifteen separate still photographs rapidly shown one after the other.

The photographs are of Tummler in various poses with his bicycle. They take up the whole screen.

SOLOMON (V.O.)
Tummler sees everything. Some say he's downright evil.
He's got what it takes to be a legend. He's got a marvelous
persona.

*The snapshots finish and we see Tummler and Solomon speed ahead
on their bikes.*

A black cat is sitting on the sidewalk licking itself.

*Tummler and Solomon slam on their brakes. Both of their back
wheels slide in the gravel. They stop a few feet in front of where the
cat is sitting.*

The black cat pays no attention.

Tummler grabs his BB gun.

SOLOMON
You got this one?

TUMMLER
Yes.

Tummler points his gun directly at the cat.

SOLOMON
Wait up. It's gotta neck leash. Don't kill it. It's got a thin
neck leash.

The black cat looks up at the gun and then takes off.

It runs up the front yard of the house.

*Tummler continues to aim his gun at the cat as it runs up the neatly
manicured lawn.*

The black cat stops on the front porch and stares at the two boys.

Tummler looks disappointed as he puts his rifle down to his side.

He continues to watch the cat.

TUMMLER
You know what I'm gonna do tomorrow?

                              SOLOMON
What?

                              TUMMLER
I'm goin' to an insane asylum.

                              SOLOMON
An insane asylum?

                              TUMMLER
I'm gonna get me a ravin' beauty.

Tummler turns his head and smiles deviously at Solomon.

They both ride away.

EXT. WIGGINS HOUSE – DAY

*The front of the house is neat and proper. It is small and quaint.
There are no plants, only a wooden porch swing.*

*There is a yellow above-ground swimming pool in the center of the
front yard.*

*The house is exactly like the rest of the houses on the street: lower-
middle class and depressing.*

The wind is blowing and leaves are falling.

*Darby, a nine-year-old girl, walks out onto the porch and grabs the
cat with both hands.*

*Darby is small and skinny. Her hair is dark and so are her eyes. She
is missing several of her front teeth. She has a cute crooked grin. She
is wearing a tight Cookie Monster shirt and a pair of cut-off jean
shorts. She's not wearing any shoes and her feet are dirty. She has
dirt around her mouth.*

She picks the cat up and squeezes its stomach.

                              DARBY
Foot Foot, where have you been?

She smells Foot Foot's neck.

You smell like a dooky, girl.

She turns around and quickly walks into the house.

INT. WIGGINS HOUSE – DAY

Darby walks through the door.

There is a large coat rack on the side with an oval mirror going up the center. There are many coats hanging on it. There are three pairs of multicolored plastic rain boots sitting neatly at the bottom.

In front of the mirror is a big bowl of licorice and gummy bears.

Darby, still holding Foot Foot, picks up the bowl of candy.

Foot Foot shakes around.

Darby squeezes her tightly around the neck and begins to run straight up the steps.

She runs up the wooden steps. Her feet make a loud slapping noise.

Foot Foot is being held by the neck.

When she gets to the top step she pushes Foot Foot up with her knee so that she has a better hold.

We hear the sounds of girls singing.

INT. DOT AND HELEN'S ROOM – DAY

Dot and Helen are standing with their backs facing the camera. They are simultaneously marching in place and doing a cheer.

The room is medium-sized. There are two small water beds sitting next to each other in the center of the room. On each bed, there is a large pink pillow with the two sisters' names neatly embroidered.

A small chandelier hangs from the top of the ceiling. A pink plastic tape recorder sits on top of a large wooden dresser drawer with a huge round mirror.

There is a picture of Foot Foot taped to the mirror. A large glittery heart outlines the picture.

*On one of the walls is a mounted swordfish with the name Clarence
Clearwater scribbled on its side.*

*Both girls are wearing cheerleader outfits and waving brightly col-
ored pom poms. They both have bobby socks on their feet.*

*Dot is eighteen. She has completely white hair and eyebrows. Her
face is round and pretty. Her eyes are as blue as the bluest sky. She
has several rings on her fingers. She is about 5'5" tall. Her accent is
strange and she has trouble pronouncing certain words. She speaks
with a made-up accent.*

*Helen is sixteen. She looks exactly like her older sister, only she is a
few inches shorter. She is a smaller version of her older sister. She
wears silver braces.*

*Darby runs and opens the door with Foot Foot and the bowl of
candy.*

Helen and Dot jump around and continue to scream and cheer.

They wobble their butts from side to side.

Darby drops Foot Foot on the floor.

> DOT
> (*screaming*)

Foot Foot! You stinker bitch.

Dot and Helen both drop their pom poms onto the floor.

Dot drops to her knees and starts caressing Foot Foot.

She looks a little impregnated.

> HELEN

Flip her over and look at her bottom private.

Dot turns Foot Foot onto her back and starts counting her nipples.

Helen sits down beside her.

Is it red?

> DOT

It's not red.

HELEN

Is it any swollen?

DOT

No.

HELEN

An impregnated cat is a bitch. An unwed Calico is a sin if
she gets impregnated.

DOT

She still has nine nipps.

Darby is chewing on a large red licorice stick.

DARBY

Nine nipps.

HELEN

Nine lives too.

INT. DOT AND HELEN'S ROOM — NIGHT

Dot and Helen are standing in front of their mirror.

*They both have their shirts off. They are both wearing black-and-
green striped bicycle shorts. They both have bobby socks on their feet.*

*Darby is standing on the corner of one of the beds. She is wearing
an electric blue jump-suit with the feet built in, and one of the feet
has been torn off. She is watching her sisters and throwing her fists
up towards the sky. She is jumping up and down on the bed.*

Dot breaks off a piece of thick black electrical tape.

She sticks it on one of her nipples.

DOT

See, do it like that. It has to be done on it tight.
(*pats the tape*)
Get it over all the pink around it.

Helen is watching closely.

                              HELEN
      But tight you can get it infected.

Dot does the same thing to her other nipple.

                               DOT
      Don't tell me. This is the right way. If you just do little
      pats it won't raise it. The whole point is to make it fatter.
      And to pop it out bigger.

Dot pats the tape down.

She raises both her hands above her head and turns towards Helen.

      Pull 'em off. Do it quick. Do it quick.

                              HELEN
      How should I do it?

                               DOT
      Do it quick.

Helen bites her bottom lip and puts her hand on the corner of the tape.

*Darby is jumping up and down and slapping both her hands
together. She is watching and laughing.*

                             DARBY
                     (*screaming with excitement*)
      Do it quick, Helen. Pull it.

Helen rips the tape off Dot's breast.

Helen makes a nervous grumbling noise.

                               DOT
      Didn't hurt.

Dot drops her arms and turns to look at herself in the mirror.

                              HELEN
      It looks bigger.

                               DOT
      It looks an inch. About an inch bigger. It looks wider. The
      width looks fatter.

HELEN
It looks redder too. I think it looks much better.

Dot looks down at her breast and smiles.

DOT
A better nipple.

Darby starts cracking up.

CUT TO:

Dot and Helen are jumping up and down on their bed.

They both have big black pieces of tape covering the fronts of their breasts.

The Buddy Holly song 'Everyday' is playing on the record player.

The girls are running around their room singing the song.

Darby is jumping up and down in the corner. She is dancing with a long silver baton. She is screaming the words to the song.

As the song continues the girls' voices become less and less distinct. Finally we cannot hear anything else except for the song, which is playing at full volume.

All three of the girls continue to dance and do gymnastics. They are all smiling and having fun.

The next thing we see is Dot jumping up and down on her bed in slow motion.

The song has stopped and there is no background noise. The only thing we hear is Dot singing the chorus to 'Everyday.' It should sound as if it were taped on a micro-cassette recorder.

DOT (V.O.)
(*singing alone*)
Every day it's a gettin' closer, goin' faster than a roller coaster, love like yours will surely come my way, hay hay, hay hay hay hay . . .

EXT. DIRT ROAD — DAY

Tummler and Solomon are crouched down on the side of a small dirt road. Their bikes are lying down beside them.

Solomon is holding a floppy dead cat in his hand. He is holding it by its back legs.

He stands up and starts twirling the dead cat around in circles.

Tummler is holding a large garbage bag. It's about a quarter of the way filled with dead cats.

Solomon tosses the cat but it misses the bag and hits the ground.

Tummler gracefully bends down and sticks the dead cat in the bag.

> TUMMLER
> What do you wanna do?

Solomon raises his shoulders and makes a funny face.

> You wanna keep lookin'?

Tummler and Solomon stand.

Tummler puts the bag in his backpack and then zips it up.

> Go up by Dean's place, up back by the dumpsters.

> SOLOMON
> No.

> TUMMLER
> Then let's get our money.

> SOLOMON
> Let's get some milk shakes.

> TUMMLER
> Milk shakes?

> SOLOMON
> A strawberry milk shake. If they don't have strawberry, I'll get pineapple.

TUMMLER
Let's go get our money first.

They both straddle their bikes.

Does your mom ever make you food?

SOLOMON
She makes me toast.

TUMMLER
Is that all?

SOLOMON
She cooks me lamb chops.

TUMMLER
Have you ever eaten a crêpe suzette?

SOLOMON
No.

Tummler stares at Solomon.

He spits a few feet from Solomon's shoe.

She also makes good cheese melts. She makes good
cheese melts.

They ride away on their bikes.

EXT. SUBURBAN STREET — DAY

The two boys are riding their bikes.

Tummler stands up on his bike and starts doing little tricks.

He does little bunny hops and pop-o-wheelies.

The sound of wheels turning gets very loud.

TUMMLER (V.O.)
(*solemnly*)
This banker had gravy on his vest. Gravy on his tie. Gravy
on his pants. Gravy all over him. So he went to his grave,
with gravy on his vest. Gravy on his tie. Gravy on his

pants. Gravy all over him. That dirty old man.

He does a big wheelie and smiles.

Solomon puffs his cheeks out.

INT. BENCH — DAY

Two menacing teenage skinhead brothers are sitting next to each other on a wooden bench. They both have red hair, and one of the brothers has a swastika tattooed onto his forehead. They both have their shirts off and are laughing.

We hear some slow, gloomy death-metal music played at a low volume.

> ANONYMOUS CARTOON VOICE (V.O.)
> After the tornado hit, in the town next over from Xenia, these two skinhead brothers murdered their parents. They both claimed to be raised as Jehovah's Witnesses.

SUPER 8 FOOTAGE – *of hundreds of stray cats running around.*

> Then for some reason there seemed to be a million cats running around everywhere.

A dead cat is washed up in the sewer and flies are buzzing around its head.

> Some of 'em just died on their own 'cause they couldn't get enough food to go around.

A close-up of one of the skinhead brothers spitting into the lens of the camera.

INT. HUNTZ'S GROCERY STORE — DAY

Huntz, a heavy-set middle-aged black man, is standing in the middle aisle of his grocery.

There are no customers present.

Old-time music is playing on the radio.

Huntz is wearing brown corduroy pants and thick bifocals. He has a gold cross necklace around his head. He is wearing a white button-up dress shirt. He has a round, friendly face.

Tummler and Solomon walk in through the front door. Small bells are hanging from the door knob.

They both look at Huntz.

They put their rifles down by the entrance door.

> TUMMLER
>
> Hi, Huntz.

Huntz nods.

We hear the voice of a young girl from across the room.

> REBERTA (O.S.)
>
> Daddy, how much is nine times seven?

> HUNTZ
>
> Forty-nine.

Huntz shakes his left arm up and down.

He begins to walk to the back of the store.

The two boys follow.

Reberta, a skinny ten-year-old black girl in a yellow sun dress, is sitting behind the cash register writing in a school notebook. She is Huntz's daughter. There are several stains on her dress.

> TUMMLER
>
> Hello, little Reberta.

Reberta looks up. She is missing one of her front teeth.

> REBERTA
>
> Hi, Tummler. You got somethin' for me?

> TUMMLER
>
> A few.

Huntz walks back behind the counter and into the storage room.

The boys follow.

Tummler walks in first.

Solomon stops and looks at Reberta.

Reberta looks back at him.

Solomon puffs his cheeks out and crosses his eyes.

Reberta sticks her tongue out.

Solomon walks in.

INT. STORAGE ROOM – DAY

The room is filled with all sorts of boxes and hanging food products.

In the middle of the room is a large hanging scale. It sits above a wooden table. Behind the scale is a small silver freezer with the word 'ice' painted on it.

A bunch of mops and brooms rests in the corner.

There is a long metal cooler to one side.

Huntz walks behind the scale.

Tummler takes his backpack off and retrieves the plastic bag from inside.

He hands the bag to Huntz.

> HUNTZ
> You didn't get very many.

He puts the bag on the wobbly scale.

> TUMMLER
> No. It's a scarce count.

Tummler itches his nose.

> HUNTZ
> Twelve pounds.

He looks closely at the shaking scale.

> Twelve and a half. Say thirteen.

Huntz picks the bag up and throws it in the freezer.

                          TUMMLER
It's gettin' crazy now 'cause things are starting to thin out.

                          SOLOMON
Tummler almost killed a house cat. But I saved its life.

Huntz opens up a spiral notebook and writes in it.

                          HUNTZ
You've got competition.

                          TUMMLER
What da ya mean? Who?

                          HUNTZ
Jarrod.

                          TUMMLER
Who?

                          HUNTZ
Jarrod Wigely. He lives by the school. He takes care of his
grandmother.

                          SOLOMON
I know that kid. He used to have a sister in my class but
she moved. Her name was June Wigely. They used to call
her June Bug 'cause she looked like a June bug.

Solomon makes a face in an attempt to imitate a June bug.

                          TUMMLER
I know the boy. He hangs at the playgrounds, right?

                          SOLOMON
That's the one.

                          TUMMLER
Brown shaggy hair.

Huntz nods.

SOLOMON

Yep.

HUNTZ

He comes in almost every day.

TUMMLER
(*looking devious*)

Does he?

HUNTZ

I don't see so many cats any more. They ain't in the trash
like before. And the one Chinese restaurant that was
buyin' these things from me . . . The guy . . . The owner,
he just died of a heart attack so it'll probably be out of
business soon anyway.

He pulls out a wad of cash from his back pocket.

TUMMLER

I'm pretty smart, if I say so myself.

Huntz looks up at him.

HUNTZ

Why's that?

TUMMLER

Well, this afternoon I went into a fruit store an' the clerk
thought I was some kind of out-of-town hick. But I fooled
him.

HUNTZ

How?

TUMMLER

'Those two apples will cost you two dollars each,' he tells
me. That's when I outsmart him. I hand over a five-dollar
bill. As he's about to give me a dollar change, I say, 'Keep
it, we're even. On the way in I stepped on a grape.'

Tummler smiles.

Huntz chuckles.

Solomon has no reaction.

Huntz looks at his money.

HUNTZ

You want it per cat or per pound?

TUMMLER

It don't matter.

HUNTZ

A dollar on the pound.

TUMMLER

Deduct two pints of glue too. OK?

Solomon smiles.

HUNTZ

What kind?

TUMMLER

Not wood glue . . . Not cement glue either. You have
Butchers model glue in the tins?

HUNTZ

Yep.

INT. HOUSE — DAY

VIDEO FOOTAGE — *an anonymous boy, aged seventeen, is sitting on
a red couch next to a midget.*

*The anonymous boy is wearing a brown sweater and black-rimmed
glasses. The midget is wearing a pink turtle-neck sweater and silver
ballet slippers.*

ANONYMOUS BOY
(screaming at the top of his lungs)

I was born right here in Xenia, Ohio, to a lesbian midwife
who parted her hair over to one side . . . My mom has
huge stretch marks . . . And as a child I used to roll mar-
bles on her belly . . . She entered menopause in her late
thirties and this made my sister nervous because she

might take after my mother and sprout a moustache and
lose all her drive for living.

                    MIDGET
I am a fucking midget. I'm short and that sucks and I hate
myself. I am also gay, so life seems doubly as hard. Once I
was on TV, and just for that reason I am considered the
most famous fucking short guy. I hate life. People trip me
all the time and hold me up by the rib cage. Just 'cause I
am short that means all my friends have to be short, which
means I have very little selection. I try to be friendly and I
think about drugs a lot. My mom played high-school basketball so I always asked myself, what the fuck happened
to me?

The anonymous boy starts to laugh like a hyena.

The midget leans over and punches him in the arm.

INT. DAIRY QUEEN – DAY

*Strawberry milk shake drains out of a big metal machine. It is fill-
ing up a large cup.*

A girl in a Dairy Queen uniform puts a plastic lid on top of the cup.

She retrieves a straw from underneath the counter.

She smiles and hands Solomon the milk shake.

EXT. DAIRY QUEEN – DAY

There are a few cars parked in front of a shabby Dairy Queen.

*In one of the cars, there is a sleeping woman behind the driver's side.
The window is rolled down and country music is playing.*

Solomon and Tummler are sitting on their bikes next to the entrance.

Solomon is joyfully drinking his milk shake.

*Tummler is picking the front of his bike up by the handlebars. As he
does this, he makes a noise like a motorcycle.*

EXT. DRAINAGE DITCH — EVENING

Tummler and Solomon are sitting under a little backwoods bridge, reclining in an empty drainage ditch.

Trash and empty wine bottles are scattered everywhere. There are also playing cards thrown all over. A few pairs of dirty sneakers are hanging from atop the bridge.

Every once in a while we can hear a car slowly rumble over the bridge.

The wind is blowing.

Tummler opens the lid of glue and pours it into a see-through plastic bag.

Tummler hands the bag to Solomon.

Tummler picks up another plastic bag and fills it with glue.

The two boys put the bags up to their faces and start breathing in and out.

The bag fills with air and then the boys suck the fumes out and it quickly deflates.

We watch them do this for about a minute or so.

They put the glue sacks down.

Both of their faces are bright red.

Tummler flicks Solomon's ear and laughs.

> SOLOMON
> (*rubbing his earlobe*)

Oww! Darn.

> TUMMLER
> (*smiling*)

Ear ache.

He sets his head back and smiles.

Solomon is stoned out of his mind.

Tummler wipes his eyes clean.

Solomon rests his head next to Tummler's.

Did your mom find a new house?

SOLOMON

No.

TUMMLER

I saw a house yesterday, by my house. I think it was this
lady's . . .

SOLOMON

. . . Yeah.

TUMMLER

I saw a sign. For sale.

SOLOMON

Was it big?

TUMMLER

Well, yeah.

SOLOMON

What was the yard like?

TUMMLER

Well, it was big enough for you and your mom. It had a
bullet hole in the mailbox.

SOLOMON

A hole?

TUMMLER

A big ol' hole.

Solomon laughs himself silly.

I think my brother shot it there when I was younger, a
long time ago. I think it was him. He used to say Roy
Orbison liked to shoot at stuff, an' Roy always wore dark
sunglasses and my brother always wore the same kind of
sunglasses.

Solomon makes the sound of a gun going off.

He sang that song, 'Cryin'.' You know that song.

SOLOMON
What?

TUMMLER
That song, 'Cryin'.'

Solomon says nothing.

Tummler sings the chorus of the song.

There is silence for a moment.

Tummler rubs his eyes.

Solomon sticks his pinky finger in his ear and moves it around.

Tummler breathes into the bag again and coughs.

My brother used to sing 'Cryin'.'

SOLOMON
Where's he now?

TUMMLER
My brother?

SOLOMON
Yeah.

TUMMLER
He's in the big city. He took off in a bus.

SOLOMON
Yeah?

TUMMLER
Yeah. He's a queer. He's a queer now.

SOLOMON
Your brother is?

TUMMLER
He dressed like ladies. You know? He wears skirts and lip-

sticks. He wears stockings and eye liner.

SOLOMON

Does he wear those girls' shoes?

TUMMLER

He wears red ones. He even has boobs.

Solomon chuckles.

I got a postcard from him. He sent me this postcard. It said he changed his name to 'Hot Sissy.' An' I hid it away from Daddy 'cause there was a picture of him on the front and he was all bent over and shit. He was tryin' to look all sexy.

SOLOMON

What did he look like?

TUMMLER

Like a . . . pretty much he looked like a girl. His hair was long and curly.

SOLOMON
(*smiling*)

A girl?

TUMMLER

Pretty much like it.

SOLOMON

Was he pretty?

TUMMLER

I don't know . . . I guess.

He thinks for a second.

I guess so. I'm sure he has a boyfriend. I'm sure he's pretty enough to have a boyfriend. He said he had one.

SOLOMON

I'll bet he's pretty. In a dress and all. And lipstick.

Solomon picks up the glue sack and starts inhaling.

He does this for a while and then puts his head back down next to Tummler's.

INT. COPS SEGMENT

STOCK FOOTAGE – *a two-minute video segment from the television show* Cops.

The scene revolves around a blond-haired teenage boy who gets caught sniffing paint. He has paint all over his face.

His father paces back and forth asking himself what he should do about his son.

The son stands in front of his mirror making faces and smiling.

EXT. SUBURBAN STREET – DAY

The sounds of birds chirping is magnified.

We see the same skinny twelve-year-old Bunny Boy from the opening credits. He is still wearing pink rabbit ears. He is wearing Bermuda shorts, no shirt, and a pair of velcro sneakers.

He is riding his yellow skateboard down the middle of the street.

He rides from side to side.

A little ways down the street, we see two nine-year-old boys shooting each other with cap guns.

Both boys are wearing cowboy hats and cowboy boots. They both have gun holsters around their waists. They are standing on a manicured lawn. One of the boys has a split lip.

As they shoot their guns at each other we hear loud pops go off.

The boys are laughing and screaming.

The Bunny Boy continues to ride his skateboard down the street.

The Bunny Boy looks up at the two boys playing.

He gets off his skateboard and walks up onto the sidewalk in front of where the two boys are playing.

The Bunny Boy stands there and watches the kids shoot each other.
He is holding his skateboard under his arm.

One of the boys kicks the other in the shin with the side of his boot.

The Bunny Boy just stands there watching, motionless.

The two boys turn and look at Bunny Boy. They just stop and stare.

All three just stare at each other.

                    LITTLE BOY I
    Shoot the rabbit.

Both the boys start shooting their cap guns at the Bunny Boy.

Bunny Boy falls down like he's dead. Half of his body is on the side-
walk, the other half is lying in the street. His skateboard is in the
street.

The two boys look happy.

                    LITTLE BOY 2
    I got him.

                    LITTLE BOY I
    I got him first.

                    LITTLE BOY 2
    No you didn't.

The two boys run up to where Bunny Boy is lying.

They look at him closely.

Little Boy I kicks him in the side of the leg.

Bunny Boy remains motionless.

EXT. TENNIS COURT — DAY

Eddie, aged fifteen, is hitting a white tennis ball against a wall.

He has very fair skin and short blond hair. He is wearing tennis
shorts and high-top sneakers without socks.

Dot and Helen are watching him from behind a chain-linked fence.

HELEN

He got a hair cut.

DOT

I know.

HELEN

Do you think it looks good?

DOT

It looks much better than before.

HELEN

Yeah.

DOT

He looks pretty.

HELEN

His thighs are gettin' stronger.

Eddie misses the ball and it bangs into the fence.

He looks over at the girls and smiles.

He twirls his racket and walks over to the girls.

EDDIE

Hi, Dot, hi, Helen.

HELEN

Hi, Eddie.

DOT

Hi.

Eddie stops in front of the fence. They begin to talk to each other through the fence.

EDDIE

My backhand really sucks.

DOT

No.

EDDIE

Yeah, it does.

DOT

Your playin' looks better.

EDDIE

Thanks. I got second at a tournament last week.

DOT

Yeah?

EDDIE

Yeah. My serve got faster. It increased by eight per cent. I can hit a ball sixty-five miles an hour.

HELEN

You got that way from practicin'?

EDDIE

No, I got this thing called ADD.

The girls look at him.

It's an attention disorder. It affects the nervous system.

HELEN

Yeah?

EDDIE

It makes it hard to concentrate.

DOT

It makes it hard?

EDDIE

It makes it hard, 'cause like when I would play before I knew I had ADD, I would just kinda half-way go for the ball. I wouldn't run the extra mile.

HELEN

Yeah.

EDDIE

But like, it's hard to explain. I take Ritalin, this kinda pre-

scription drug. It's not like a drug that fucks you up. If
anything it makes you normal.

DOT

I didn't notice it before.

*We see an image of Eddie running in place with his racket. He has
an intense expression on his face.*

EDDIE

Yeah, well, it was more to do with the way I felt. I was
anti-social. That's why I stopped goin' to church.

DOT

You couldn't take any more, right?

EDDIE

No, I would just be nervous. Like my legs would shake
and hit the pews and stuff.

The girls smile.

My parents thought that I was just causin' trouble. It
wasn't really my fault.

He looks at the two girls and grins nervously.

EXT. SUBURBAN STREET – DAY

Dot and Helen are casually walking down a neighborhood sidewalk.

HELEN

He just likes to go out with skinny girls.

DOT

How do you know?

HELEN

I just know.

DOT

Who told ya?

HELEN

'Cause his last girlfriend used to be an anorexic.

                              DOT

Was she a bulimic?

                             HELEN

I don't know.

                              DOT

She was probably a puker. A bulimic puker with white
spots on her teeth.

                             HELEN

I knew it was his girlfriend 'cause she used to run track
after school. And this girl said, 'Oh, that skinny girly is
Eddie's girl.' And I thought, 'What for? That girl is so
skinny.'

                              DOT

But they broke up?

                             HELEN

A while ago.

They walk silently for a while.

                              DOT

Skin and bones.

                             HELEN

She used to wear rubber bands around the tops of her
socks. She used to wear a belt around her spandex bike
shorts to keep 'em up.

EXT. FRONT YARD — EARLY EVENING

VIDEO FOOTAGE — *a chubby girl in her mid- to late teens is hanging
by her neck from a short tree.*

*She has apparently just hung herself to death. She is dressed only in
a black bra and panties. She is wearing one striped tube sock, and a
dog is hurriedly licking the ball of her other foot. Her long hair covers most of her face.*

We hear a previously recorded conversation. The sound is very bad.

It should sound as if you were playing a cracked tape that you found on the side of the road.

ANONYMOUS OLDER MAN (V.O.)
Ritchie, stop teasing that girl.

ANONYMOUS BOY (V.O.)
Why? She's a dirty ass ho' bag. I'll stop when I'm ready.
I'll date rape her when I'm ready too. She's a liar. I hate
that bitch.

The sound of people screaming in the background mixed with a loud wind.

The chubby girl is swinging back and forth from the tree. The dog follows her swaying foot.

ANONYMOUS OLDER MAN (V.O.)
No. No, don't do that.

ANONYMOUS BOY (V.O.)
I throw her down the steps and kill her baby. She's a liar.
She told me that the whole time I was in juvenile prison,
that she wouldn't sleep with no one. Then I just told her
to fuck off and lose some weight.

Close-up of the dog licking the heel of her foot.

The sound of people yelling in the background and a few birds chirping merrily.

EXT. CHILDREN'S PLAYGROUND – DAY

It's cloudy outside and the wind is blowing. It looks like it's getting ready to be dark.

Solomon and Tummler enter the gates of a small beaten-up playground.

The playground is filled with teenagers hanging out. There are no children present.

People are sitting on wooden benches drinking beers and smoking cigarettes. There are more boys than girls.

Everything is pretty much trashed and written on.

Words are carved into the wooden benches: 'Randy loves Tonya, '83,' etc.

People are running around and talking.

A shirtless boy has his arm around a white girl with big hair.

Solomon and Tummler make their way through the park, pushing their bikes. They look silently at all the teenagers hanging out.

As they walk through the park, we begin to focus on a group of boys sitting on the top of a picnic table.

We watch them in slow motion as they drink, smoke, laugh, and look mean.

The song 'Rocket Man' by Elton John is playing.

The slow motion ends.

The music softens.

The boys on the bench start laughing at something.

One of them takes his high-top sneaker off and smells it.

> BOY
> (*holding his shoe*)
> Smell this shit, dude.

Tummler and Solomon walk over to where two boys are sitting on some swings.

They stop a few feet in front of the boys.

The boys look at them.

There is a pause.

> TUMMLER
> Are you Jarrod Wigely?

> JARROD
> (*nods*)
> Yeah.

Jarrod is seventeen years old. He has shaggy brown hair that flops down in his face. He's wearing a Kenny Rogers T-shirt and a pair of jeans with holes in the knees. He has a small radio on his lap. He is listening to the song 'Rocket Man.' He has a kind of innocence about him.

Sitting next to him is a nineteen-year-old mulatto boy named Karl, with puffed out hair and a cast on one arm. He is wearing glasses. He is also smoking a cigarette with the same arm that has the cast. The cast is dirty and there is a bunch of writing on it. He has no laces in his shoes.

There is a small pool of watery mud beneath their feet.

> TUMMLER

You know Huntz?

> JARROD

Yeah.

> TUMMLER
> (*slowly*)

Well, I spoke to Huntz and he told me some stuff about you.

> JARROD

What did he say?

> TUMMLER

He said that you've been killing cats.

> JARROD

Cats?

> TUMMLER

He said so.

> JARROD

Yeah, a little bit.

> TUMMLER

A little bit?

> JARROD

For about the last three weeks.

TUMMLER
When do you go out? You do it during the day usually?

JARROD
No, I do it mostly at night.

TUMMLER
You shoot 'em?

JARROD
No, I put glass in tuna fish. Or mostly I sprinkle poison
around the dumpsters. In the corners and back by the
church.

He points his finger.

They pause and stare at each other.

Jarrod looks around and pops his knuckle.

You're Tummler, right?

TUMMLER
(*deadpan*)
Yep.

JARROD
And you're Solomon.

Solomon nods and smiles proudly.

*Jarrod looks at the ground and kicks it lightly with the heel of his
foot. He seems nervous, like he's thinking of something to say.*

He begins to say something but stops himself.

Tummler just stares at him.

Karl blows out a steady stream of smoke.

Well, look, I'm sorry if you're mad . . . It wasn't like . . . It
wasn't like I was tryin' to fuck with you or anything.
(*looks up*)
I was like . . . you know . . . I needed the money and shit
. . . It seemed easy enough.

TUMMLER

Huntz said that you take care of your grandmother.

JARROD

Yeah, she's sick.

TUMMLER

How old is she?

JARROD

I'm not sure . . . She's probably about . . . I don't know,
ninety or ninety-one.

TUMMLER

You bathe her?

JARROD

I usually scrub her off with a big sponge.

*Solomon is standing to the side with his arms crossed and his bike
resting between his legs.*

TUMMLER

You have to change her diaper?

JARROD

Yeah, I hate doin' that shit. I hate all that shit.

SOLOMON

Does she speak to herself?

JARROD

No, she don't speak. She's catatonic. She used to speak to
herself. She'd watch game shows all the time and yell out
stuff to herself.

KARL

She used to throw darts.

JARROD

Yeah, she used to have a dartboard.

TUMMLER

What happened to your parents?

JARROD

My parents . . . they both went to prison.

TUMMLER

They went to prison?

JARROD

When I was younger. I was a little kid.

TUMMLER

What for? What'd they go in for?

KARL

Robbery.

JARROD

Yeah, robbery. They stole TV sets.

TUMMLER

TV sets?

JARROD

Yeah.

KARL

They did armed robbery too, right?

JARROD

No, they robbed a restaurant. But they didn't have any weapons. It wasn't armed.

He looks at Tummler.

Tummler says nothing.

Jarrod looks back at the ground and then coughs into his hand.

TUMMLER

So, now you just take care of your granny?

Jarrod shrugs.

JARROD

Yeah.

> TUMMLER

You kill cats too.

> JARROD

Yeah.

Solomon laughs.

Tummler smiles.

EXT. FIELD – DAY

VIDEO FOOTAGE *– of a chubby fourteen-year-old boy. He's wearing a tight blue sweatshirt and a pair of army pants. He's got a pair of black rain boots on.*

He's standing in the middle of a field.

He's got a long rake in one hand, and in the other hand he's grabbing a fluffy white sheep by the tail.

The boy is laughing for no apparent reason.

The sheep is trying to get loose.

The boy keeps screaming, 'Get the sheep, get the sheep.'

> ANONYMOUS BOY (V.O.)
> (*young sounding*)

My friend Kenny used to play games with whoever was around. Sometimes he would play too rough and injure his friend. When he got older he had a weight problem, and I could tell he was embarrassed because he wouldn't take his shirt off at the beach. His grandfather sent him to an abandoned island and told him to get skinny. He told me he had fun on the island. He said there were lots of things to do.

The boy lets go of the sheep and begins to swat it with the rake.

INT. COLE'S HOUSE – LIVING ROOM – NIGHT

Solomon and Tummler are staring into a large fish tank. We hear the squeaky voice of Cole, screaming from upstairs.

COLE

Come on up.

Tummler and Solomon raise their heads from the fish tank.

Cole's house is nice and big. It is decorated in a bland upper-middle-class way. The carpet is gray, there is a piano in the corner, a nice fireplace, and a glass table with magazines.

There is a carpeted stairway next to the fish tank.

Tummler walks up the stairs.

Solomon looks closely at the fish tank.

He taps the tank window with his knuckle and then takes off up the stairs.

INT. COLE'S HOUSE – UPSTAIRS ROOM – NIGHT

Cole is standing at the top of the stairs. He's about seventeen years old and has a mean face. His hair is blond and shaved except for the back, which is long. He is wearing one small earring, a red sleeveless T-shirt with little holes in the shoulder, and long shorts and house slippers. He has a large build. His eyes are blue.

The room is full with bookshelves and a big television. There are two large chairs facing each other at opposite ends of the room.

There is a door on one side of the room, next to the stairs.

Tummler walks up and then Solomon follows.

TUMMLER

Hi, Cole.

They shake hands.

COLE

Wassup, man?

TUMMLER

Nothin'.

Cole puts his hand on Solomon's shoulder.

COLE

Did you ride your bikes here?

TUMMLER

Yeah.

COLE
(*smiles*)

You brought some money?

TUMMLER

Yep.

Cole looks at Solomon.

COLE

You too?

Solomon nods.

Solomon and Tummler pull money out of their pockets.

Solomon pays all in one-dollar bills.

She had a migraine headache this morning, so she almost
wanted to call it off. I gave her a bunch of aspirin.

Cole smiles. His teeth are dirty.

*They hand Cole the money and he puts it in his pocket without
counting it.*

Cool . . .

Solomon and Tummler look at each other.

Solomon points at Tummler.

TUMMLER

I'm going to see her now.

He wipes his forehead with the side of his sleeve.

COLE

Hold up.

Cole walks over to the door and sticks his head inside. He talks quietly but we can still hear him.

> You ready? . . . Yeah . . . Put that bathrobe thingy on . . .
> Yeah . . . Put it on.

He pulls his head out and shuts the door.

> She's ready.

He looks at Tummler.

> You're goin' first?

> TUMMLER
> Yeah.

Tummler opens the door and walks in.

Cole follows behind and sticks his head in.

> COLE
> Leave the lights on . . . Yeah, leave that one on too . . .
> Cassidey.

Cole closes the door tightly behind him.

Solomon sits down in the big chair.

> You want a cigar?

> SOLOMON
> No.

> COLE
> My dad's got a box of Cubans.

Cole walks to the other side of the room and opens a drawer full of files and papers.

He pulls out a cigar box from underneath.

He opens the lid and grabs a thick cigar.

He picks up an ornate silver lighter from the bookshelf and begins to puff.

He starts blowing smoke rings into the air.

Solomon is watching Cole.

Cole looks at the ceiling.

There is a moment of silence as we watch Cole smoke like a pro.

We follow the smoke rings upwards until they disappear.

> SOLOMON
> Did your girlfriend cut her hair?

> COLE
> Yeah. She chopped it off to her shoulders. In a bob.

> SOLOMON
> I thought so.

> COLE
> Why?

> SOLOMON
> I saw her yesterday.

> COLE
> Where was she?

> SOLOMON
> Downtown.

> COLE
> Where?

> SOLOMON
> She was at some plant store. I think she bought a little
> Grandfather cactus.

Solomon pops a stick of striped chewing gum in his mouth.

> COLE
> Who was she with?

> SOLOMON
> I think she was with her mom and some friends.

                              COLE
Any guys?

Solomon shakes his head 'no.'

    We almost broke up. We did break up for a day but then
    we sorta got back.

Solomon chuckles.

    She's like a little devious bitch.

Solomon laughs.

    But she had all these problems when she was a kid and
    shit. She was abused.

                            SOLOMON
                           (*smiling*)
She was beaten up?

                              COLE
More sexual abuse than anything.

                            SOLOMON
I voted for her for cheerleading.

                              COLE
You did?

                            SOLOMON
Yeah.

                              COLE
I think she's an awful cheerleader.

Solomon laughs.

                            SOLOMON
She always looks sad. She's a sad cheerleader.

                              COLE
Her moves always suffered. They were lower.

He kicks his leg out.

Her leg kicks were all low and shit.

SOLOMON

Yeah.

COLE

That's 'cause her dad was abusin' her.

Solomon smiles.

Cole kicks his leg out further.

That's why her leg kicks were all low.

Solomon laughs lightly.

Cole blows out a big stream of smoke.

Then he walks to the glass table in the center of the room and rests his cigar on a big crystal ashtray.

The smoke continues to stream upwards.

You want a drink or anything?

SOLOMON

No thanks.

COLE

Some rum? If you want, I got some rum in the back.

SOLOMON

No.

Cole walks out of the room.

Solomon remains sitting.

Solomon pulls a thin black plastic comb from his back pocket. He quickly combs his hair over to one side so that it is completely flat.

Cole walks back in holding a chair.

Solomon puts the comb back into his pocket.

Cole walks up to the door and puts the chair down.

Then he grabs his cigar and takes a few quick puffs.

Cole climbs onto the chair and begins to peek through a small crack in the top of the door.

What are you lookin' at?

Cole is silent for a moment.

COLE

When Cassidey was younger she used to feel weird about her looks. I mean, no one ever told her she was pretty. And she entered puberty real early and I guess she liked boys, but who knew what they thought of her.

Solomon looks down at his belt and then undoes it and takes it in one hole.

She used to go to, like, the expensive women's clothing stores at the shopping mall and she would try on these expensive dresses so that the girls who worked in the stores would tell her how pretty she looked in the dresses. You know they would; they would want her to buy the dress, obviously, 'cause they make a commission off that shit. She would just go in there so that she could hear those women tell her how pretty she was.

Cole steps off the chair and takes a big puff of his cigar.

He walks over and puts the cigar back in the ashtray.

Then he grabs his chair and walks back out of the room.

The door opens. Tummler walks out with a somber look on his face.

He closes the door behind him.

Cole walks back into the room.

Tummler sits down on the other big chair.

Solomon stands up.

Cole walks over and opens the door. He sticks his head in.

(*quietly*)

You ready?

Tummler begins to put his shoes on.

Solomon walks over to the door.

(*still with his head in the door*)

... OK.

He closes the door and walks away.

Go on in.

INT. CASSIDEY'S ROOM – NIGHT

The room is decorated very simply. There is a big poster of Christie Brinkley on the wall. There are a few pictures of Cassidey and her brother Cole on her desk.

Solomon walks in.

Cassidey is sitting on the side of the bed. Cassidey is a nineteen-year-old girl with Down's syndrome. She has a pretty red bow in her hair. Her lips are caked with red lipstick. She is wearing a flowery nightgown. She has a big smile on her face.

We hear the sound of a music box playing faintly in the background.

CASSIDEY

Hi, Solly.

SOLOMON

Hi.

CASSIDEY

Are you clean?

Solomon nods.

Did you use soap?

Solomon nods.

Let me smell your wrist?

Solomon sticks his wrist out and Cassidey sniffs it.

Solomon sits down next to her on the bed.

It smells good.

Solomon looks excited.

> SOLOMON
> How does it smell like?

> CASSIDEY
> Like fruit. Like cherries.

> SOLOMON
> My mom gives me cherry shampoo.

> CASSIDEY
> I like cherries. I like cherries on my ice cream. I like the
> name Cherry. Cherry.

There is a pause.

Cassidey is holding Solomon's hand.

You have hands like a girl.

> SOLOMON
> No, I don't.

> CASSIDEY
> Yes, you do.

Solomon makes a face.

I can read your fortune.

She begins to look at Solomon's palm.

This big line says you're gonna be a millionaire. It says
your wife is gonna die in a fire.

> SOLOMON
> I don't have a wife.

> CASSIDEY
> You will though . . . and it ain't gonna be me.

She laughs and gives Solomon a little peck on the cheek. It leaves a red lipstick mark.

Solomon looks embarrassed.

> SOLOMON
> Do you wanna go swimmin' tomorrow?

> CASSIDEY
> No, I don't.

She starts laughing.

> (*pointing to his cheek*)
> You have on cute lipstick.

> SOLOMON
> Do you have a bikini?

> CASSIDEY
> No, silly.

INT. COLE'S HOUSE – UPSTAIRS ROOM – NIGHT

Tummler is standing in the middle of the glass table doing a comedic monologue.

He is waving his arms up and down in the attempt to imitate an old-style vaudevillian.

Cole is sitting in the big chair laughing hysterically. He has a cigar in one hand and a glass of rum in the other.

The song on the music box continues.

Tummler is wearing only one shoe.

> TUMMLER
> Folks, my timing is off lately. When I set down to eat, I get sexy. When I go to bed, I get hungry. People are crazy these days! I saw a man lying in the street. I said, 'Can I help you?' He said, 'No, I just found this parking space and sent my wife to buy a car.' It's just murderous what's going on with people today. One fellow comes up to me

on the street right here in Xenia and says he hasn't eaten
in three days. I say, 'Force yourself.' Another guy comes
up and says he hasn't eaten in a week. I say, 'Don't worry,
it tastes the same.'

Cole puts the cigar in his mouth and starts to clap enthusiastically.

All right, we're rolling! I love this crowd!

INT. CASSIDEY'S ROOM – NIGHT

*Cassidey is lying down on the bed. Her head is propped up by a
bunch of pillows.*

Solomon is at the other end of the bed, massaging her foot.

*Cassidey picks up a glass of water from the nightstand and takes a
sip.*

*We hear a previously recorded conversation playing on top of the
image.*

> SOLOMON (V.O.)
> Uh, I used to swim at summer camp. I used to wear a
> garbage bag in the rain. That was the first place I got
> drunk.

> CASSIDEY (V.O.)
> The Bible says drinking is a sin. So is being famous.

> SOLOMON (V.O.)
> Sometimes I worry about those things. Most of the time I
> don't believe in heaven.

Solomon is digging into her foot.

> SOLOMON
> Does that hurt?

> CASSIDEY
> No.

She puts the glass back on the table.

Solomon begins to massage her Achilles tendon.

EXT. ABANDONED FIELD — DAY

We see a dead cat hanging from the branch of a tree. Its back legs are tied together with thin string.

Solomon and Tummler are standing next to each other, whipping the cat with long twigs.

As they do this, the cat swings limply back and forth.

Solomon is wearing a red fireman's hat and dark sunglasses.

EXT. BACK-ALLEY DUMPSTERS — NIGHT

Jarrod is crouched down next to a giant dumpster.

There is trash and crap all over the place.

Flies and bugs are swirling around.

Jarrod has a dirty red book bag next to him.

He grabs a piece of crumpled-up newspaper from beside him.

He flattens it out.

He takes an orange Tupperware bowl out of his book bag.

He opens it and dumps a large portion of tuna fish onto the newspaper.

He pulls a plastic sack full of broken glass out of his bag and then dumps some of it into a pile of tuna.

Then he retrieves a small container of cream and pours it on top.

He mixes it all together with an old wooden spoon.

He makes a face while he does this because the odor is so intense.

EXT. GAS STATION — DAY

Solomon and Tummler are standing in front of a gas station.

They are repeatedly shooting a dead cat with their BB guns.

An old pick-up truck drives by and beeps its horn.

They continue to shoot, one after another.

Every time they shoot the cat, it moves a little from the impact of the BB.

Solomon and Tummler look very serious as they do this.

EXT. STREET IN FRONT OF DOT AND HELEN'S HOUSE — DAY

Dot, Helen, and Darby are all roller-skating around in circles.

They are playing some sort of game.

They are laughing.

> HELEN
>
> You're it!!!

Dot and Helen are wearing matching Catholic-school dresses.

Darby falls down on her butt.

EXT. DOT AND HELEN'S FRONT PORCH — DAY

The sun is shining, and leaves are blowing across the front of the house.

Dot and Helen are sitting on a wooden porch swing.

Darby is sitting on her knees painting Dot's toenails pink.

The birds are chirping.

A dog barks loudly from next door.

Helen turns her head and looks annoyed.

> HELEN
> (*talking to the dog*)
>
> Shut up!

> DOT
>
> I hate that dog.

> HELEN
>
> I hate it too. It's mean and ugly.

DARBY

It has two sets of teeth like a shark. That's why Roy calls it Sharky.

HELEN

Yesterday I saw it eatin' a turkey bone and it looked like it was chokin' on the bone.

DOT

I wish it had. I wished it would choke up to death an' shut up.

HELEN

That's the only time it didn't look mean, when it looked ready to die. And I was gonna go run over and tell Miss Berry but . . .

DOT

. . . After last time?

HELEN

But after last time I didn't even wanna get near to her front door.
(*imitating an old lady*)
'You kids get out my yard are I'm callin' the police.' She said the word 'are.' 'Are I'm callin' the police.'

DOT

Go 'head, you old bag.

DARBY

You want glitter on your toes?

DOT

Hell no.

DARBY

You don't want sparkles?

DOT

Hell no.

The dog continues to bark frantically.

EXT. SIDE OF THE ROAD — DAY

Solomon is shooting a stop sign with his BB gun.

Tummler is sitting on his bike smoking a cigarette.

INT. SOLOMON'S HOUSE — KITCHEN — DAY

The kitchen is small and connected to the living room. There are dirty dishes in the sink. The wallpaper is brown and yellow flowers.

Solomon walks into the kitchen.

His hair is slicked back and he is not wearing a shirt. He is wearing tight blue jeans and long white tube socks that are falling off his feet.

He has a roll of masking tape around his wrist.

He opens a drawer full of silverware and pulls out all the forks and spoons.

He separates them carefully into two even sections.

He picks up both sections and wraps tape around them tightly. They each become a makeshift barbell.

Solomon walks out of the kitchen.

INT. SOLOMON'S HOUSE — BASEMENT — DAY

Solomon clicks the light on. The room becomes very bright.

Solomon walks down some creaky wooden stairs.

He is holding the barbells in one hand and a medium-sized radio in the other.

The basement is rather large. There is a wall-length mirror on one side. The floor is hard and scuffed-up. There are boxes and piles of old clothes lying on the floor. On the wall is an old movie poster of Cab Calloway doing a split in mid-air.

The basement is like a combination dance studio and storage space. Solomon walks to the end of the room and sets the radio on the floor.

He presses the 'play' button and turns the volume all the way up.

The Madonna song 'Like a Prayer' comes blaring out.

Solomon walks in front of the mirror. He is holding a silverware weight in each hand.

He begins to pump iron with the forks and spoons.

Madonna song: 'I hear your voice, it's like an angel crying. I have no choice, I hear your voice.'

We hear his mother scream from upstairs.

SOLOMON'S MOTHER
Solomon, are you down there?

Solomon says nothing. He just looks at himself in the mirror.

Solomon's mother walks down the steps.

She looks exactly like Solomon. She is very tall and skinny. Her hair is bleached blonde, and about two inches of her roots are jet black.

Her eyebrows are plucked thin and penciled in. She is wearing nylon gray pants and a white blouse. Her bra is visible through the shirt. She looks like she's lived in a broom closet for the past thirty years.

What are you doing lifting weights?

SOLOMON
I'm liftin'.

She looks at him in the mirror.

SOLOMON'S MOTHER
You're gonna stunt your growth with those things. You're gonna get peg leg shoulders and pinched neck nerves.

She walks toward the radio.

Solomon continues to lift.

She bends over and lowers the volume.

It's not good to lift while you're growin'.

She looks at him from across the room.

I can see your shoulder popping out . . . Look . . . The way it raises and gets smaller.

Close-up of Solomon's shoulder.

It's going to pop out of joint. That's not healthy. Look at it. It's gonna pop.

He is so thin that you can almost see his heart beating through his skin.

Solomon makes an angry face in the mirror.

Solomon's mother looks at a stack of clothes and then bends over and picks up a huge pair of men's black patent leather tap shoes. They look like they're size fourteen.

Your dad's old taps.

She stares at the shoes.

He used to be good. He said he was blessed with the gift of tap. He took up tapping when he got his bald spot. He wanted to get transplants, but I thought that was a bit drastic.

Solomon turns to the side and looks at himself in the mirror while he continues to lift.

Solomon's mother sits down on a chair.

I told him if he wanted to, he should take up tap.

She puts her hands inside the shoes and begins to bang them on the floor.

He put the mirror up and he got excellent. He said that if Raquel Welch could see him dance, that she would fall in love.

She smiles in a bashful way.

She takes her shoes off and then slips her feet into her late husband's tap shoes.

She stands up and looks in the mirror.

> (*talking to herself like she's remembering the*
> *conversation word for word*)
> What do you want with Raquel Welch? She had her bot-
> tom ribs surgically removed so that she would have a more
> hourglass figure. Don't you know that stars are flawed?

She starts dancing.

She waves her hands in the air like a nervous ballerina.

Solomon pays no attention to his dancing mother.

Her shoes are falling off her feet, but she continues to dance.

Solomon lifts his weights and looks in the mirror.

Solomon's mother spins around on her toes.

The music gets very loud as we watch the two of them in the mirror.

INT. BATHROOM – DAY

Bunny Boy walks into a public bathroom and examines himself in the mirror.

He pulls a small frog from out of his pocket.

He puts the frog up to his face and examines it closely.

He pulls a rubber band out of his pocket.

He pulls an M-80 fire cracker out of his pocket. 'It' has an extra long fuse.

Using the rubber band, he wraps the firecracker tightly around the stomach of the frog.

The frog is squirming and kicking.

Bunny Boy puts the frog in the sink.

He bends down and lights the fuse.

He stands up and walks away.

The frog starts jumping around and croaking.

The M-80 goes off and the frog explodes.

INT. DOT AND HELEN'S HOUSE – BATHROOM – DAY

The bathroom is large and brightly colored.

The sound of water coming out of the faucet is magnified.

We see three different colored toothbrushes neatly hanging from a dispenser on the wall. The names of each girl are written separately on the brushes.

Dot and Helen are giving their cat Foot Foot a bath in the sink.

Darby is in the background using a toilet.

She is reading a motorcycle magazine.

Helen is holding Foot Foot down as Dot adjusts the knob.

HELEN

That's too cold.

Dot turns the heat up.

That's good.

Dot picks up a bottle of shampoo and pours it on Foot Foot.

DARBY (O.S.)
(in the background)

I want a moustache, damn it!

The girls begin to furiously lather up Foot Foot.

DOT

Watch her eyes.

They flip Foot Foot on her back.

HELEN

Rub her underbelly.

DOT

Her under booty.

She laughs.

HELEN

Get her nipples.

They pour soap onto Foot Foot's stomach.

DARBY

Damn it! Damn it!

Darby is still on the toilet. Only now she is sticking her tongue out of a picture of Burt Reynolds winking. He has a huge moustache in the picture.

Darby is sticking her tongue out of his mouth.

DARBY (V.O.)

Damn it! I want a moustache.

She wiggles her tongue up and down.

Damn it!

The sound of water ceases.

Dot and Helen are gently drying Foot Foot off with a cream-colored towel.

INT. HOUSE – DAY

FOUND HOME-MOVIE FOOTAGE – *of a man and a woman wrestling each other on the carpeted floor of their living room.*

The carpet is an ugly orange color. There is a thin blue wrestling mat in the center.

A slightly balding man in nothing but tight orange gym shorts is being put into a head lock by a heavy-set brunette woman with long brown hair. She is wearing an orange-and-blue striped bikini.

They are fighting each other like mad.

We hear the voice of an anonymous boy. He sounds like he is in his early teens.

ANONYMOUS BOY (V.O.)
My parents would fight each other in front of their
friends. 'Bring me the towel, Mamma's lip is busted. Bring
me a white towel so we can remember the stains.'

*The woman is sitting on top of the man. She is shoving her elbow in
his face.*

*There are about five other people standing in the room smiling and
cheering. They are all wearing bathing suits.*

Sometimes Dad would say how much he wanted to break
her pelvis off. 'I'll kick it off. I'll bust it off its hinge. A
powerful man can pop a woman's pelvis in a quick kick.
With the heel, not the toe. The toe will get stubbed.'

*The man is now sitting on the woman's stomach. He has her hands
pinned to the ground.*

She is trying to break loose.

Sometimes Momma's tit would fall out and Dad would
start laughing. And all the friends would look around and
start laughing.

*The woman is behind the man, choking him with a thick, white
leather belt.*

*This entire scene is done lovingly, like an organized sport. Everyone
in the room is laughing and smiling.*

INT./EXT. CAR – DAY

Tummler and his father are driving slowly down the street.

*It is raining mildly and the sound of the windshield wipers scraping
against the glass is loud.*

Tummler's father is driving a ten-year-old brown Pontiac.

*He looks about fifty-five years old. He has curly gray hair and a big
stomach. He has a funny round face, like a cute doll. He is wearing
a faded blue blazer with suede patches on the elbows. His voice
sounds like a little kid's.*

Tummler is sitting on the passenger side. He is wearing a dirty mesh baseball cap with the brim folded in the shape of a 'V.'

Between them is a bouquet of roses.

> TUMMLER

Do you still miss her?

> TUMMLER'S FATHER

Not a day goes by that I don't think about her.

Pause.

> TUMMLER

It seems that way sometimes.

> TUMMLER'S FATHER

Not a single day.

> TUMMLER

You think she looked like me a little bit?

> TUMMLER'S FATHER

She looked a little bit like you.

> TUMMLER

She's in heaven now.

> TUMMLER'S FATHER

Yes, she is.

Tummler's father slows down at the stop sign.

He puts the turn signal on and it makes a clicking noise.

Tummler puts the air conditioner on.

He adjusts the vents so that it points in his direction.

INT. TUMMLER'S ROOM – DAY

Tummler is sitting at his desk.

There are papers scattered everywhere. There is a framed picture of Eddy Cantor on his desk. On the wall in front of his desk is a picture of Jimmy Durante smiling, with the word 'Shnozzola' at the bottom.

Tummler has his shirt off and his hat on.

He turns his desk lamp on and begins to write in a spiral notebook.

He turns the radio on at his desk. Classical music comes out. It is very dramatic sounding.

As he writes, we hear him speak the words.

The camera focuses on the letters being written on the page, the way the pen moves, and the shape of his letters. Very close up.

> TUMMLER (V.O.)
> His dad never gave a crap, not even at the end of his game. It was scary to see him despondent like that. His dad didn't care for Mom much either or the little doggy. He started going to church. And he started listenin' to the gospels. It was expected when he robbed the neighbors. He took their wine and he took some rings and fine jewelry. I think he got a fur coat as well. When he had a kid, he didn't think to watch his ways. He thought the same as his daddy.

Tummler sets his pen down and looks at his writing.

He scratches his ear lobe.

Close-up: he picks up his pen and marks two lines through the word 'daddy.'

He clicks the light off.

INT. TUMMLER'S HOUSE – KITCHEN – NIGHT

Tummler and his father are sitting opposite one another at a small poker table with a brown checkerboard tablecloth.

There is a plastic squeeze bottle of ketchup on the table. There are several cans of empty beer scattered everywhere.

There is a third man present in the room. He looks like he's in his late twenties. His shirt is off and he has a medium-sized beer gut. He has long curly blond hair that is parted neatly down the center and patches of facial hair. He is wearing thick black bifocals that make the size of his eyes look magnified. On his wrist he is wearing a multicolored bracelet.

Tummler and his father are also shirtless.

They are all three drunk and laughing.

The third man is standing up with a beer can in his hand.

He is singing a song and doing a little dance.

This scene should feel as if we entered in the middle of something.

THIRD MAN

Come on then . . . Put your . . .

TUMMLER'S FATHER

. . . Shut up . . .

THIRD MAN

. . . Put your elbow up on the table . . .

TUMMLER'S FATHER

. . . I'll put my elbow up on your head . . .

Tummler puts his elbow on the table.

TUMMLER

Let's go . . .

THIRD MAN

. . . Let's go.

TUMMLER'S FATHER

Where to . . . Where are we goin' . . . Albuquerque, New
Mexico?

THIRD MAN

I already been there . . .

TUMMLER'S FATHER

So . . . Go on back the way you came in.

THIRD MAN

Look . . . Look here, I told you, man. Put your elbow up
on the table.

Tummler's father smiles and then starts rubbing his shoulder.

He sips his beer.

. . . Put it up.

The third man continues singing and dancing.

Tummler's father puts his elbow on the table and jingles his fingers.

Tummler and his father grasp hands.

> (*laughing*)
> Whoo! . . . Fuck his ass up, Tummler.

TUMMLER'S FATHER
OK . . . Tell me when . . . When you're ready.

Tummler smiles and nods.

The third man puts his hands on top of theirs.

THIRD MAN
Amarks, get sets . . .

Tummler smiles.

GO!

Tummler and his father begin to arm wrestle.

The third man starts to sing at the top of his lungs.

Tummler's face looks like the devil.

His father starts making strenuous noises.

Tummler starts pushing his father's hand down.

> (*laughing*)
> You got 'em.. .You got 'em, Tummy.

His father tries to push his hand back up.

Take 'em out . . .

Tummler smacks his father's hand to the table.

TUMMLER'S FATHER

Shit!

TUMMLER

Whoo!

They all three start laughing.

TUMMLER'S FATHER

Damn, you got strong.

Tummler's father starts massaging his own shoulder.

THIRD MAN

Told ya.

They all continue to laugh.

Tummler's father stands up and drinks his beer.

He starts spinning his arm around.

Tummler is watching his father.

You got old . . . Old man.

TUMMLER'S FATHER

Shit.

The third man opens a beer, and then the fuzz comes shooting out and onto the floor.

THIRD MAN

It's a immortal . . . A moral sin to get beat by your son . . .

The third man sits down in the chair and starts to laugh.

. . . Don't you know that?

EXT. SUBURBAN STREET – DAY

We see the back of Bunny Boy as he skateboards down a hill with his arms pointed out to the sides.

EXT. SIDEWALK — DAY

Solomon and Tummler are riding their bikes around downtown Xenia.

They ride past cars, stores, and a few stray pedestrians.

The general atmosphere of the town is small and depressing. Most everyone looks worn and poor.

Both the boys have their BB guns around their shoulders.

As they ride around, we see them looking for stray cats.

They are checking around the dumpsters.

They crouch down and look in the bushes behind the dumpsters.

Solomon picks up a handful of gravel and throws it against the side of a dumpster.

Tummler kicks one of Jarrod's home-made cat traps.

SOLOMON

I don't see any.

The two boys look depressed.

SUPER 8 FOOTAGE — *of a cat licking its crotch.*

INT. TUMMLER'S ROOM — DAY

Tummler and Solomon are sitting next to each other on the bed.

The bed is propped up against the wall. They are both leaning against the back wall.

They are both breathing in and out of paper bags. Tummler is holding a small vial of White Out in his hand.

As Tummler breathes in the bag, he puts his thumb over the top of the White Out and shakes it back and forth.

Solomon has one of his socks off and he is cleaning the cracks of his toes with his finger.

The window is open and the wind is blowing the curtains wildly.

Tummler is wearing big sunglasses.

The sound of birds chirping is heard.

INT. HOSPITAL — DAY

The redhead girl from the opening scene is sitting in a drab hospital room.

She is wearing a white hospital robe.

There are a few people sitting down in chairs around her. Her eye make-up is smeared.

The room is filled with a few flowers and hanging balloons.

She is looking at the floor.

A bright red balloon in the shape of a heart is tied to her wrist.

> ANONYMOUS TEENAGE GIRL 1 (V.O.)
> She got breast cancer. They had to take out one tit. On her left side.

> TUMMLER (V.O.)
> Which one was she?

> ANONYMOUS TEENAGE GIRL 2 (V.O.)
> She was the redhead. The ugly one with the unicorn tattoo.

The redhead girl turns to one of the people in the room.

> REDHEAD GIRL
> *(looking totally miserable)*
> The doctor says he's gonna have to take off one of my boobies and I know what happens when they do that: the boys stop lookin' at you or once when you finally get a boy that you like he'll see your scar and then just stop talkin' to you for no reason. Boys are like that. I know.

> ANONYMOUS TEENAGE GIRL 1 (V.O.)
> She finally convinced her father to let her have plastic surgery. She began to write poetry about her feelings, but no

one wanted to listen 'cause she looked so bad.

> ANONYMOUS TEENAGE GIRL 2 (V.O.)
> I felt sorry for her but I still never wanted to talk to her
> 'cause she made me sick to look at.

Close-up of the redhead girl rubbing her eye.

EXT. HUNTZ'S GROCERY STORE — DAY

Huntz's daughter Reberta is standing in front of her father's store.
She is wearing a dress and holding a small ukulele in her hand.

Solomon and Tummler are standing in front of her on their bikes.

> REBERTA
> All the cats are gone. You guys killed 'em all. You extermi-
> nated all the strays.

> TUMMLER
> Is your dad here?

Reberta shakes her head 'no.'

> REBERTA
> He went to get me a dress for the Little Miss Pageant.

She starts hitting the strings on her ukulele.

Solomon makes a face.

> Jarrod came by yesterday an' dropped off the last two cats.
> He said they were the last two strays in town.

> TUMMLER
> The last two?

> REBERTA
> One of 'em had blue dye in its fur. An' Daddy said that
> the cat with dye died.

Tummler and Solomon ride their bikes away.

Reberta starts strumming her ukulele and marching in place.

INT. JARROD'S HOUSE – KITCHEN – NIGHT

It is very dark and all the lights in the house are off except for the one in the hallway that casts a bit of light into the kitchen.

Solomon enters through the window.

He is wearing a Dolly Parton mask with long curly blonde hair.

He squeezes through and then falls to the floor.

> TUMMLER
> (*from out the window*)

Here.

Tummler hands Solomon a golf club and a BB gun.

He climbs through the window.

He is wearing the same Dolly Parton mask. He has his backpack on.

> (*whispering*)

Come on.

They quietly walk out of the kitchen.

Jarrod's house is small and junky. Stuff is thrown everywhere. Everything is broken and dirty. All the couches and chairs are ripped. All the rooms are connected.

As they walk through the house, they start flipping the lights on behind them.

INT. JARROD'S ROOM – NIGHT

Tummler walks in and hits the light switch.

Jarrod's room is a total pig sty. Everything is on the floor and broken. A paper-thin mattress is half falling off a spring bed. His clothes and food bowls are on the floor. Empty cigarette packs and ashtrays are everywhere. The place looks worse than terrible.

Tummler looks around.

Solomon walks in after.

SOLOMON

Jarrod ain't here.

Tummler walks out of the room. He is holding a golf club.

Solomon is wearing a BB gun around his neck.

He starts looking around the room.

He kicks some junk on the floor.

He looks at the dresser and sees a few pictures of Jarrod standing in his underwear posing like a bodybuilder. The last picture is a close-up shot of Jarrod smiling and holding a large pistol to his own head.

Solomon sets the pictures down and picks up a pair of clean, folded, white tube socks.

He sits down on the squeaky mattress.

He kicks his shoes off.

He then pulls the dirty gray socks off his feet. They are way too big for him and they have huge holes in them.

He puts the clean white socks on his feet.

He pulls them up over his knees.

He tosses the gray socks to the floor.

He puts his shoes back on and then stands up.

He walks over to a stack of porn magazines sitting on the edge of a cluttered desk.

He begins to flip through them.

He folds one up and stuffs it under the front of his shirt.

His elbow hits the stack of magazines and they slide off onto the floor.

He looks down at one of the magazines and then carefully picks it up.

Tummler walks into the room.

TUMMLER

Solomon!

Solomon jumps. He is holding the magazine in one hand.

He looks up at Tummler.

SOLOMON
(*deadpan*)

He's got a gay one.

Solomon is holding a gay porn magazine.

TUMMLER

Come on.

Tummler walks out of the room.

Solomon drops the magazine onto the floor and then walks out of the room.

INT. JARROD'S GRANDMOTHER'S ROOM — NIGHT

We see a close-up of Jarrod's grandmother's face. She looks like a ninety-year-old living corpse. She is comatose. There are tubes sticking in her nose. Her lips are blue and she is grinding her teeth together on one side. The sound is loud and repetitious. It's as if someone is chewing chalk.

We watch her grind her teeth.

We see her feet at the end of the bed. They are neon white and her toenails are long and brittle looking.

Tummler and Solomon enter the room. They are still wearing their masks.

Solomon walks up and looks at her.

She is on a respiratory machine. The machine is on a small table by her bed.

Solomon looks closely at her face.

SOLOMON

Is she dead?

Tummler walks over and pulls her eyelids open.

TUMMLER

She's alive on that machine.

SOLOMON

She stinks.

TUMMLER

Her life is over.

SOLOMON

She smells like a baked ham.

Tummler picks up her arm and then drops it on the bed.

TUMMLER

I bet she could live like this for ever.

SOLOMON

You think she'll ever wake up?

TUMMLER

Hell no. She's dead as hell. Go over and shoot 'er in the
foot.

SOLOMON

Why?

TUMMLER

Try and wake 'er up. Shoot her in the foot.

Solomon walks over and points the rifle at her foot.

He pauses for a moment and then fires one in.

It makes a dull noise but her body does not respond.

SOLOMON

I shot her in the ball of the foot.

TUMMLER

I told ya she's dead.

He looks at the machine.

You can live for ever on one of these gadgets.

We watch Jarrod's grandmother grind her teeth. Tummler clicks the 'off' switch on the life-support system.

SOLOMON
She'll be dead now.

Tummler bends down and pulls the plug out of the socket.

TUMMLER
She's always been dead.

She stops grinding her teeth.

She's been gone for a while.

Solomon looks at her.

SOLOMON
She sure stinks.

We see a close-up shot of a BB lodged in the heel of her foot.

INT. COFFEE SHOP – DAY

The coffee shop is old and relatively empty.

There are flies buzzing around and a cook behind the counter scrambling eggs.

There is only one waitress present.

There are three teenage delinquent boys sitting side by side at the end of the counter.

They all look dirty and malnourished. Their hair is greasy and messed up. Their clothes are torn and tattered. One of the boys has very crooked teeth, another boy is wearing two wrist watches on the same arm. The third boy has lines shaved into his eyebrows.

A short old lady with balding hair and orange-painted fingernails is sitting at the other end of the counter eating rice pudding and drinking coffee. She has a small hole in her throat from getting a tracheotomy.

The boys are all putting cream and sugar into their cups of coffee.

DELINQUENT BOY 1

I had a lot of trouble.

DELINQUENT BOY 2

Yeah.

DELINQUENT BOY 1

Like, I don't know. It was weird. You know, my mother
and dad never got married.

DELINQUENT BOY 2

Yeah.

DELINQUENT BOY 1

I think in a strange way it kinda fucked me up, ya know?

DELINQUENT BOY 2

I'm sure it did. When I got caught stealin' for the first
time, I was like, I don't know. I was like eight or nine or
some shit. And the psychologist was all like, 'Oh shit, it's
'cause my mom couldn't even remember who the hell my
dad was.' You know?

DELINQUENT BOY 1

Yeah.

DELINQUENT BOY 2

She like had no idea and shit. She probably got drunk and
shit and fucked some dude who, like, she didn't even
know or anything.

DELINQUENT BOY 3

It's always like that. 'Cause before, people used to just
fuck and fuck. Like truck drivers and shit. My mom told
me she fucked some guy in a car and like, who knows, you
know. That could have been my father. She just stood
there in front of the car wash and just fucked dudes.

*The old lady at the end of the bar looks over at the three boys drink-
ing their coffee.*

Her voice sounds like Darth Vader.

                    OLD LADY
                   (screaming)
        Will one of you BASTARDS pass the cream?

The three delinquent boys look at her.

A clump of rice pudding is falling off the edge of her lip.

INT. PUBLIC REST ROOM – DAY

The Bunny Boy is sitting on a toilet playing a small blue accordion.

He is tapping his foot.

We hear someone flush the toilet in the next stall.

EXT. K-MART PARKING LOT – DAY

The sound of a cat screaming.

Close-up of a paper flyer flapping on the windshield of a parked car.

The flyer reads, 'MISSING BLACK CAT, AGE 3, BLUE EYES, MY PAL FOOT FOOT.' The words 'Foot Foot' are in big black lettering at the top of the page. There is a xeroxed picture of Foot Foot in the center.

                    DOT (O.S.)
        Have you seen Foot Foot?

                    HELEN (O.S.)
        Foot Foot, where are you?

                    DARBY (O.S.)
        Kitty kitty kitty. Meow, meow.

EXT. K-MART IN FRONT BY THE ENTRANCE – DAY

We see Dot and Helen standing by the automatic doors.

They are handing flyers out as people enter and exit. They look sad and panicked.

Dot is speaking to an old man in a wheelchair. He has a sack of groceries on his lap and is wearing an orange scarf.

OLD MAN
I don't like cats.

DOT
(*looking ready to cry*)
It has short black fur. If you see it, go like this.
(*makes a Mickey Mouse voice*)
'Here, Foot Foot. Here, Foot Foot.' Then it'll probably
jump on your lap. You just hold it tight around the stomach and then call my number. OK, mista?

Dot puts one of the flyers inside the man's bag of groceries.

The old man makes a face and then rolls himself away.

*Darby is standing a few feet away, looking at the small toy and
candy vending machines. She is playing with the knob and talking
to herself.*

Helen is speaking to a middle-aged married couple.

HELEN
It disappeared last night. It's never stayed out all night.

The middle-aged couple just nod.

She'll just lick your fingers to death. And if your fingers
are dirty then it'll get a disease. Wash your fingers if you
find her.

INT. K-MART FOOD COURT – DAY

People are sitting around eating and talking.

Darby, Dot, and Helen are quietly sitting at a table.

Each one of them is eating a corn dog.

They look sad and out of luck.

A pile of missing Foot Foot flyers are sitting on the table.

                              DOT
You want mayonnaise, Darb?

                             DARBY
No.

We see a deaf couple in the corner arguing.

                              DOT
Those people are deaf.

                             HELEN
I bet she's cussin' him out.

We watch the three girls scarf down their corn dogs.

A bald man wearing a green V-neck sweater walks up to where the girls are sitting.

He is holding one of the flyers in his hand.

                           BALD MAN
Is this your cat?

                             DARBY
Yeah!

                           BALD MAN
Well, I know where it is.

INT./EXT. BALD MAN'S CAR – DAY

The bald man is driving the three girls.

Dot and Helen are both sitting in the front seat. They are sharing a seat belt.

Darby is sitting on her knees in the back seat. The bald man is driving an expensive sedan.

                           BALD MAN
My brother was Freddy Prince. You know who that is?

                              DOT
No.

BALD MAN

He was in a television show called *Chico and the Man*. Did you ever see it?

DOT
(*shaking her head*)

Uh-ah.

BALD MAN

He was an actor.

HELEN

What do you do?

BALD MAN

What do I do?

HELEN

For a livin'.

BALD MAN

I write gossip. I write for a newspaper.

HELEN

You write gossip?

BALD MAN

Yes.

The car gets quiet for a second.

You know gossip?

DOT

No.

BALD MAN

Sid Caesar used to paint his toenails red like his mother. Did you know about that?

HELEN

No.

BALD MAN

Warren Oates used to swallow his chewing tobacco spit.

Placido Domingo likes sherbet ice cream. Steppin Fetchit is the founder of MENSA. Debbie Gibson has rickets. Adolf Hitler only had one testicle.

Darby has her face pressed against the window.

DARBY
(*interrupting and excited*)
. . . Look, that girl's on stilts!!!

We see a girl walking down the sidewalk with large wooden stilts. She is wearing a Michael Jackson jacket and one white glove.

Darby turns around and looks at her from out the car window.

No one else notices.

As we watch the girl on stilts walking down the sidewalk, we hear the bald man continue his list.

BALD MAN (O.S.)
Elizabeth Taylor is a beer enthusiast. P. T. Barnum had an ulcer the size of a small oyster. Henry Winkler is allergic to papayas. Satchel Page shot heroin in Cuba. Oppenheimer drank rubbing alcohol.

We return to the car.

BALD MAN
Patrick Swayze saves all his old ballet slippers in a cardboard box marked 'fragile.'

DOT
I don't know that stuff. I didn't know it.

BALD MAN
Those are rumors.

DOT
That's what you get paid for doin'?

BALD MAN
I get paid for rumors. Yes, it is.

HELEN

Darby's little friend Chloe is related to Barbara Mandrell.

The bald man smiles.

BALD MAN

She almost died. Didn't she?

DOT

I don't know.

BALD MAN

In a car wreck, I believe.

HELEN

I hope Foot Foot didn't die.

DOT

Shut your mouth, bitch.

HELEN

You're a bitch.

DARBY

You're boff stinker bitches.

HELEN

You.

The bald man starts laughing.

He comes to a stop light.

How much further is where you saw Foot Foot?

BALD MAN

I'm not sure. It's around here . . . Around here somewhere.

HELEN

Where?

*The bald man looks down at Dot and Helen's legs. They are both
wearing matching Catholic-school dresses.*

BALD MAN

It's around here. Can you hand me the map?

DOT

Where?

BALD MAN

Under there.

He points to the floorboard on the passenger side. Dot puts her hand down.

It's under the seat. Hold on.

He undoes his seat belt and leans over to where the girls are sitting.

He drops his hand down and it rubs against Helen's inner thigh.

Where is it?

He brings his hand back up the same way.

Dot and Helen look at each other.

DOT
(angrily)

Why'd you try an' touch her coochie?

Dot throws open the door.

BALD MAN

I'm trying to get the map.

DOT

The map ain't in her coochie.

HELEN
(screaming)

Get out the car, Darby!

Darby opens the door and gets out.

Helen takes her fist and smashes the bald man in the head.

Dot leans over and pops him in the face.

They start screaming at him.

The bald man starts yelling back.

Dot and Helen get out of the car and slam the door.

They start walking away with all the anger in the world.

The bald man speeds past them and almost hits them by accident.

I wish you would!!!

> DOT
> (*screaming at the top of her lungs*)
> Son of a bitch perverter. I'll make your head a rake and
> I'll plow the fields with it!!!

She grabs Darby by the hand.

The three sisters walk quickly down the middle of the street.

Helen's fists are clenched.

A few cars honk and drive around the girls.

> HELEN

Son of a bitch.

In the distance we see the girl on stilts. She is walking down the side-walk.

EXT. BENCH – DAY

The two skinhead brothers from the beginning of the film are doing chin-ups on a coat rack in the hallway.

> ANONYMOUS CARTOON VOICE (V.O.)
> The funny thing is, is that after the two boys killed their
> family they got in their car and drove to a frozen pond and
> went ice fishing.

INT. SOLOMON'S ROOM – DAY

Solomon is standing in the middle of his room playing with a paddle ball.

He is wearing only a pair of tight red gym shorts.

Every time he hits the ball with the paddle, he counts out a number.

He is standing perfectly still as he does this.

Heavy-metal music is playing in the background

SOLOMON

99, 100, 101, 102 . . .

He misses and the ball falls to the side.

He quickly resumes hitting the paddle ball.

103, 104, 105, 106.

He remains standing still as he continues to hit the ball.

INT. SOLOMON'S BATHROOM – NIGHT

The loud sound of water splashing.

Solomon's big toe is stuck inside the bath tub faucet.

We see his skinny pale leg sticking out of a soapy gray tub of water.

The bathroom is small and shabby. There is a white tile floor with hair and dirt in the cracks. The trash next to the toilet is full with paper and tissue. The sink is stained and there are old bottles of prescription medicine resting on the sink. The toilet is a few inches from the bath tub.

The bathroom door is open.

A blue toothbrush and a red toothbrush are resting in a plastic cup. The bristles are stained and worn.

There are five naked Barbie dolls strung together by their feet with dental floss. They are hanging from an empty towel holder. Some of the doll heads are missing, as well as missing arms and legs.

The sound of water splashing is very profound and distinct.

Solomon is taking a bath.

His hair is wet and slicked back.

He has a big bar of soap in his hand.

He hurriedly washes his skinny arms.

He lathers up his underarms with much determination. Then he drops his arms underneath the water.

He scoots his legs up and washes the tops of his kneecaps. Then he drops his legs.

He puts his head down and washes the back of his neck. Then he lowers his head and rinses his neck off.

He scoots down so that only half of his head is sticking out of the water. The water is totally gray and soapy.

He makes a little circle with his hand and starts spitting little bursts of water through it. He does this for a while. He starts flicking the surface of the water onto the wall.

He flicks some water onto a dirty little stain on the side of the wall. Then, with his thumb, he rubs the stain out.

Solomon's mother walks in holding a tray with a big bowl of spaghetti and tomato sauce in the center. There is also a large glass of milk and a silver fork.

She sets the tray down in the middle of the tub. It is long and it fits perfectly.

Solomon scoots back.

He picks up the fork and a stream of water falls onto the tray.

SOLOMON

Spaghetti.

Solomon's mother puts the toilet lid down and sits.

Solomon twirls the spaghetti around his fork and then puts it in his mouth.

He takes a big gulp of his milk, which leaves a stain around the top of his lip.

Solomon's mother silently watches.

She picks up a roll of toilet paper and quickly wraps a few layers around her hand.

She hands it to Solomon and he wipes his lip off.

SOLOMON'S MOTHER
Hand me the shampoo.

Solomon puts his fork down and leans over the tray of food and grabs a bottle of shampoo from the corner of the tub.

Water falls off his arm and onto his plate of spaghetti.

He hands her the bottle.

That's the conditioner. Hand me the other bottle.

He puts the bottle back and gives her the shampoo.

Solomon's mother begins to wash his hair.

Solomon continues to eat his spaghetti, while his mother massages the soap into his scalp.

A thick lather forms on Solomon's head and his mother pulls some of it off with her hands and then drops it into the water.

We watch her as she takes the bulk of his hair and twists it into a soapy pointed cone. It sticks straight up.

We hear a loud knock at the front door.

Solomon's mother stands up and wipes her hands dry on a towel that advertises Hawaiian Punch.

She walks out of the bathroom.

Solomon continues to eat.

INT. SOLOMON'S HOUSE – FRONT HALLWAY – DAY

Solomon's mother walks up to the front door and opens it.

Two eleven-year-old black boys are standing side by side on the front porch.

They appear to be twins. They are both wearing navy blue suits that are too small for them. One of the boys is wearing a small golden stud in his ear. They are both wearing white patent leather dress shoes.

One of the boys is holding a white plastic bag full of candy bars.

SOLOMON'S MOTHER

Hi.

TERRY

Hi, my name is Terry. That's my brother Phelipo.

PHELIPO

Hi, ma'am.

TERRY

Would you be interested in purchasing a crunch bar?

SOLOMON'S MOTHER

How much?

TERRY

A dollar.

SOLOMON'S MOTHER

OK.

She digs in her pocket and pulls out a dollar bill.

TERRY

The money goes to children with cancer.

Phelipo pulls a candy bar out of his bag and hands it to Solomon's mother.

PHELIPO

Also it's for Hodgkin's Disease.

SOLOMON'S MOTHER

OK.

She smiles and shuts the door.

INT. SOLOMON'S BATHROOM – DAY

Solomon is still in the bathtub.

He is chugging down the last half of his milk.

*Solomon's mother walks back into the bathroom and hands
Solomon the candy bar.*

SOLOMON'S MOTHER
Some dessert.

Solomon immediately opens the wrapper and starts eating it.

*We hear another loud knock at the front door and Solomon's mother
walks out of the bathroom.*

Solomon stuffs the whole bar into his mouth.

His hair remains standing in a point.

EXT. DOT AND HELEN'S FRONT LAWN – DAY

*Dot, Helen, and the Bunny Boy are all three standing in the small
above-ground pool.*

*Bunny Boy is still wearing his rabbit ears. Dot and Helen are wear-
ing gold swimsuits.*

Dot walks up to the Bunny Boy and smiles.

She pushes her breasts together with her hands.

DOT
You like my cleavage, Bunny Boy?

Bunny Boy nods 'yes.'

Why do you have the word 'Mac' tattooed on your fingers?

HELEN
Is that a real tattoo?

DOT
Yeah . . . It don't come off on the water.

Helen grabs his hand and rubs his finger.

HELEN
Why is it on there?

> BUNNY BOY
> (*talking very slowly*)
My parents like to call me that.

> HELEN

Mac?

Bunny Boy nods 'yes.'

> DOT
Why'd your parents name you Mac?

> BUNNY BOY
Mac spelled backwards is Cam. Cam is their favorite car.

> HELEN

Cam?

> BUNNY BOY

Camaro?

> DOT
They named you after a car?

> BUNNY BOY
They wanted to name me Plak.

> DOT

What for?

> BUNNY BOY
'Cause I was born with one fully grown tooth.

Bunny Boy hugs himself and then shivers.

> HELEN

So what?

> BUNNY BOY

My tooth was dirty.

> HELEN
Well, why do you have an anarchy sign on your wrist?

BUNNY BOY
(*smiling*)
'Cause I love fuckin' anarchy and I hate the world. I also think about suicide.

DOT
Anarchy is a form of government.

Bunny Boy smiles and then nods.

Our dad wanted to name me Eng, and Helen Chang . . .

HELEN
. . . Chang . . . Eng and Chang are the original . . .

DOT
I'm sayin' it. They were the first Siamese twins.

HELEN
From Siam.

DOT
They had twenty-six children between them. They had a female servant who lived to be 124 years old. Her name was Toowana.

HELEN
She was only four foot two tall.

DOT
She had a size sixteen shoe. Supposedly she kept the family together.

HELEN
She was the anchor of sorts.

Bunny Boy shivers.

BUNNY BOY
I wrote a poem, you want to hear it?

HELEN
Yeah.

BUNNY BOY

It goes, 'In the end we are all equal.' No way, buddy, in the end we are all finished.

Bunny Boy starts cracking up.

Get it!

Helen and Dot laugh.

You understand?

Bunny Boy continues to laugh.

EXT. MIDDLE OF A FIELD NEXT TO A ROAD – DAY

It's getting dark outside.

The clouds are out and it looks like a bad storm is coming.

The wind is blowing the branches and the trees.

Leaves are flying everywhere.

We can hear the sound of thunder and strong winds.

We see a bolt of thunder in the sky.

It seems like a bad storm is on its way.

Tummler and Solomon are shooting Foot Foot to death with their BB guns.

SOLOMON

You killed a house cat.

TUMMLER

You killed it as well.

They look at a dead Foot Foot with its legs limp and hanging to the side.

SOLOMON

Maybe it's not dead.

Tummler steps on Foot Foot's neck.

EXT. XENIA, OHIO — DAY

STOCK FOOTAGE — *we see some of the same footage that we saw in the opening scene: the famous tornado that hit the small town of Xenia.*

The sound of violent winds is the only thing heard in the background.

Houses are being smashed to pieces.

People are running around in a state of frenzy.

Trees are flying down dirty roads.

Cars are flipped upside down.

Children are crying.

The tornado smashes a supermarket into a million pieces.

The entire town is destroyed and turned inside out.

We hear the sound of a boy whimpering.

EXT. SUBURBAN STREET — DAY

A close-up of a boy's forearm.

Someone is carving the word 'XENIA' onto the pale white arm with a razor blade.

They are working on the final letter 'A.'

Blood is dripping out of the letters.

The sound of a boy whimpering in pain is heard loudly.

> ANONYMOUS BOY 1 (O.S.)
> Does it hurt?

> ANONYMOUS BOY 2 (O.S.)
> Yeah, it kills.

We see the letter 'A' completed.

The razor blade leaves the arm.

We watch the blood trickle out of the thin slices in 'XENIA.'

EXT. MIDDLE OF FIELD NEXT TO ROAD — DAY

Foot Foot is lying dead in the grass. Its pink tongue is hanging out to the side.

Bunny Boy bends down and picks it up by its neck leash.

He brings the body of Foot Foot up to his face. He is holding his skateboard in his other hand.

The storm is beginning.

We hear the wind and the trees.

EXT. SUBURBAN STREET — DAY

Bunny Boy is skateboarding down the middle of the street.

He is holding Foot Foot by its leash.

All the trees on both sides of the street are shaking violently.

It is raining fairly hard.

The storm is here.

Bunny Boy is following the yellow line in the center of the road.

His shirt is off and his rabbit ears are still on.

The lifeless body of Foot Foot shakes from side to side as Bunny Boy skates through the storm.

We follow him as he rides down the street.

julien donkey-boy

Script Structure
'Untitled'
The Screenplay

SCRIPT STRUCTURE

I. MOUCHETTE France 1966. *Dir* Robert Bresson *Scen* Robert Bresson based on *La Nouvelle Histoire de Mouchette* by

II. if I could fuck a mountain
Lord I would fuck a mountain
and I'd do it with a woman in the valley

– BONNIE PRINCE BILLY

III. An unemployed man (Chaplin) falls in love with a blind flower girl (Cherrill) and becomes involved with an eccentric millionaire (Myers), who is generous when drunk but mean when sober. After trying to earn money as a street sweeper, then as a boxer, he takes a large sum to enable the blind girl to have an operation to regain her sight. He is arrested and on leaving prison finds the blind girl cured.

IV. "The poet skims off the best of life and puts it in his work. That is why his work is beautiful and his life bad."

—TOLSTOY

V. "A work is not a series of answers, it is a series of questions . . . it is not the answer that enlightens, but the question."

—EUGENE IONESCO

VI. "God, I'm glad I'm not me."

—DYLAN, READING A NEWSPAPER ACCOUNT OF HIMSELF, 1965

Julien donkey Boy and the "Mistakist" decleration

1. i have never been one to gravitate toward the
   labelling of things. But i feel forced to declare
   my adherance to a mode of creation known as
   "Mistakism."

2. i am a "Mistakist", And all the work i produce adhers
   to the tenants attached to the Label/movement.

3. (Factors involved include.)

4. All modes of work exist to produce a single
   body of work. each faseet builds upon the other.

5. you can never differentiate between the seprate
   modes of creation.

6. A completely-unified eastlanie.

7. Mistakes are good.

8. there is no such thing as a true mistake
   only a more modern rethinking.

9. Suicide is a show of strength.

10. only in randomness and "mistakes" can one
    truely announce what is too deep to express
    in a direct and true way.

11. Football games, science projects, and explotions.

12. rather than direct a scene-document the action.

13. Provocations

14. ~~Ancestor~~ Heritage - Lineage - Prejudice.

15. grammer means more when words are
    misspelled and used ~~wrong~~ incorrectly in the traditional
    sence of the word.

16. ~~Important~~

17. Jokes without punchlines.

18. Hermits and rural Lonliness

19. A "Mistakist" must Believe in God over
    all else.

~~Dont~~

this is how i made Julien donkey Boy.

THE DOGME 95 is early "Mistakism."

'UNTITLED'

This is a nontraditional script design. The order in which the scenes are written should serve as a very broad skeletal frame. I am only using them as a guide which the story is hung upon. Because of the nature and goal of the project, the dialogue will be for the most part removed. Everything is completely warranted to change once the actual filmmaking commences. The written scenes have no particular order.

Scenes

1. Text written out in formal handwriting on black screen.
'. . . it's just that sometimes i feel disoriented.' The most perfect high-pitched dramatic peak of a female opera singer in mid-chorus should be played over the text, for a short moment, then it ceases as quickly as it began.

2. No opening credits at all.

3. A ten-year-old boy is standing all by himself in the middle of a muddy pond. He is wearing only shorts. He is covered from head to toe in mud. He is mumbling something to himself. He is holding a large kicking turtle upside down by its shell.

4. The leaves and trees sway harshly from the wind. It is magic hour and it looks as if a storm might be on its way.

5. Julien is standing on the other side of the muddy pond. He is nineteen years old. His hair is dark and curly. His eyes have almost no color in them at all; if anything, they are white and icy. He is wearing dark blue sailor pants hemmed three inches too small. He wears a tight white Oxford shirt that is also too small on him. He buttons the shirt all the way up to his neck. These are the same clothes he's worn since he was a child. He is wearing blue boating shoes that are bound together by gray duct tape; they have no laces and he doesn't bother wearing socks. He is wearing thick-lensed glasses with a wide strap that is connected to the ear pieces; they resemble Kareem Abdul-Jabbar's protective basketball goggles. This is basically what he wears throughout the film. It is like his self-imposed dress code.

6. There are eight turtles turned upside down on their backs. They are all neatly placed next to one another on the side of a

cement block that lines the edge of the shallow pond. They are
all kicking like small crying infants.

7. Julien looks around. There is absolutely no one around.

8. The sound of hard wind.

9. A slight drizzle falls on the small boy covered in mud from
head to toe. He resembles a living, moving statue that you
would be likely to see urinating water in a Greek fountain.

10. Julien walks up to the boy and begins a conversation.

11. The boy is not startled. You can tell he is familiar with
Julien. They talk for a minute about turtles. The boy says he
caught twelve in total, even though only eight are visible.

12. Julien looks around some more. He begins to cry a little bit
for no apparent reason.

13. The boy asks Julien if he wants a turtle.

14. Julien picks up the boy's tiny wooden shovel and smashes
the boy as hard as he can in the back of the head.

15. The boy falls face forward in the mud. He is not yet dead.
He makes some small useless attempt to push himself onto his
knees. He makes no sound at all.

16. Julien takes him by the hair on the back of his head and
forces the boy's face in the mud.

17. The boy is dead in the ditch.

18. The turtle the boy was holding flips itself over and disap-
pears beneath the surface of mud.

19. Julien sits on the dead boy's back and talks to himself in a

very nonchalant manner. He is crying.

20. Julien's mannerisms are a bit feminine. He speaks like a young Truman Capote.

21. Leaves are blowing.

22. Julien buries the boy in the mud using the same shovel.

23. He smashes the dead boy down with the shovel in order to make the body perfectly flush with the surface. He pounds the dead boy's skull.

24. Julien walks home speaking to himself the entire way. He is beginning to hear voices in his head. He is not sure where they're coming from. The rain is falling harder now. The mud is coming off his clothes.

25. We see an image of a baby being born. In voice-over Julien announces himself.

26. Still photos begin to flash. With every photo we begin to see Julien progress in age. He announces his age with every change of picture, from one to nineteen. The images and voice-over stop at age nineteen with a photo of him now. In the picture he is shaking the hand of a monkey at the circus.

27. Julien's father is in the basement drinking cough syrup to get high. He is waving one arm in the air. Julien's father is kind but tragic. His pants are too large for him. Even though he has a big belly, his pants are held down below his waist by a skinny tan leather belt. He is wearing white house slippers and no shirt.

28. Julien's younger brother is eating a hamburger in a White Castle restaurant. There are about twenty black people around him eating and screaming. He looks very similar to Julien except he is much more naive and boy-like. His skin is fair and

ivory, his voice is soft. He wears no glasses. He wipes a bit of
mustard off his cheek with a napkin.

29. Julien's home. It is square and normal and connected to
rows of houses that are almost all identical-looking.

30. Still images of everyone in his family. He announces the
name and age of each.

31. An old moving image of a beautiful woman in a swim cap
calmly holding a beach ball as the waves curl over her back.
Julien in voice-over: 'My mother, my mother. She was so
pretty. My mother, my mother, they lopped off her tittie. My
mother, my mother, I miss her so much. She used to hold me.
Now I can't find her anywhere, my darling little mother.'

32. Julien walks into his sister's room. She is pregnant and
beautiful. Bach is playing on a scratchy record player. She is
wearing a pink ballet outfit with a white tutu. Julien watches her
silently. She does ballet around her room, oblivious to Julien.

33. Julien is sitting silently in a bubble bath. He is wearing red
lipstick and his goggles are still on his face. He begins to smack
himself hard on the side of his head, repeatedly.

34. In his room, Julien gets dressed and picks up a rifle. He
puts it deep inside his mouth. He walks over to a picture of
Hitler that is taped on his wall. He points the gun at the photo.
He speaks to the photo.

35. Julien's brother is running up and down the stairs. He is
wearing a one-piece wrestling uniform. He has a possessed and
earnest look upon his face.

36. A small storm outside.

37. Julien is sitting on a bus drawing pictures in a notebook.
He is making a newsletter for 'Creedmore Health Care.' This

is where he works part-time taking care of people who are old, helpless, young, paralyzed, middle-aged, demented, and deformed.

38. Creedmore Hospital. An 'O'-shaped, pale green hospital.

39. Julien is standing in a huge white empty bathroom. He is hosing down five naked old men and one obese black woman in a pink bikini. He is wearing a white nurse's gown. A beautiful aria sung by Maria Callas takes over the sound.

40. A montage of Julien touching several different patients.

41. Julien's sister is looking around the inside of a children's clothing store. The saleswoman stares at her belly for a moment and then asks her if the child is a boy or a girl. She says she doesn't know yet but she thinks the baby is a boy because when the doctor did his sonogram she saw what looked like a tiny wee-wee. The saleswoman looks at her strangely.

42. Julien's sister is on her back. She is in a doctor's room and both legs are spread apart in a gynecological chair. The doctor has his head beneath her gown. He smiles at her, then removes his surgical gloves and disposes of them in the trash.

43. Julien is at his workplace. He is pushing a skinny mute boy quickly down the hallway in a wheelbarrow. The boy might possibly be older than Julien. The boy is clapping his hands together joyously.

44. One of the patients is old and gay. He cries at a picture of a boyhood crush. He begs Julien to let him apply lipstick. Julien agrees out of pity. Julien looks at himself in the mirror. He starts smacking his head. The gay man looks upset.

45. Some older patients are stumbling quietly through the hall.

46. Julien's brother goes to a local pond and watches a beauti-

ful white swan circle. He picks up a rock and tries to hit it. The swan flaps its wings. Julien's brother walks away disappointed.

47. Julien and his sister are in the living room dancing cheek to cheek.

48. The entire family is sitting around a small yellow table eating a huge water melon. They are silent for a moment, then they all begin to giggle.

49. Julien is in his room spinning around in circles. He is talking a bit of religious nonsense. His fingers are moving about the sides of his head as if he were playing a piano.

50. Stock footage of skinny Holocaust survivors in the Nazi death camps. The sound of a woman humming is all that is heard.

51. Julien speaks to a preacher in a small church confessional. He tells the preacher about all the voices that he is hearing in his head. The preacher recommends that Julien go and see a doctor.

52. A picture hanging on the wall inside of Julien's sister's bedroom. Julien in voice-over: 'My favorite piece of art is called *Cupid Complaining to Venus.*' Under the picture it reads, 'Salvation is free.'

53. Julien in voice-over: 'I also have sinful thoughts.' A lady in a nun's outfit is taking off her garter belt.

54. Julien's brother's head is caught between the thighs of another wrestler. He is in the middle of a local high-school wrestling match. He is violently pinned to the floor by his opponent. Julien's brother loses.

55. The few people that are in the crowd are all up and clapping. Julien's father stands up nervously and smiles toward his son as if to say it doesn't matter.

56. After the match there are several wrestlers in the locker room changing clothes. Julien's brother walks up to the guy that beat him and in a very kind way congratulates him and comments on how nice the medal that he won looks. All the boys laugh at him in disgust.

57. Julien's sister is in her room playing the cello badly.

58. Julien's brother tries again in vain to kill the swan.

59. Julien reads a poem he wrote to his sister. She laughs a little and makes him feel stupid.

60. All throughout the film there should be random segments that refer to lists that Julien's writing down in his notebook. For example: favorite cars, actors, girlfriends, sports, music, people, etc.

61. Julien takes old patients into a waist-high pool in the basement of the building. He and a few of the female nurses help the patients float around. Julien is wearing a swim cap. One of the other male nurses gets scolded for trying to dunk one of the older women patients.

62. One of the patients has no arms at all. He suffers from thalidomide. He drinks coffee and plays the drums with his feet.

63. A home movie shot on Super 8 is being narrated by one of the older female patients. The film is being projected in front of an audience of fellow patients. It announces the name and age of almost everyone in the hospital. It was her pet project.

64. Julien reads a paraplegic guy the letter his wife just sent him. The letter explains that the woman is requesting a divorce.

65. Julien is watching TV with the man with no arms. They are

watching the female ice-skating championships. The guy with
no arms says, 'That's called a triple axel.'

66. Julien's father asks his little brother to dress up like a girl
and dance with him. He offers ten bucks.

67. Julien's sister goes to an animal store and buys a big fat
rabbit that she calls Lumpy because it has a strange lump on
its head.

68. Julien, his brother, and his sister play with the rabbit in the
basement.

69. Julien and his siblings visit their schizophrenic Uncle Eddie
in the mental ward. They bring him a big stack of comic books
as a gift. Uncle Eddie has pissed his gray sweat pants. He talks
to them in the dialogue from the comics. He almost never
makes eye contact.

70. Julien walks home through the same windy field where he
murdered the little boy. He makes sure that the body is still
neatly concealed.

71. As he walks home Julien finds one yellow rubber shoe. He
asks out loud, 'What happened to the other one?' He looks
around and continues to walk.

72. Julien drinking from a water fountain inside of a hospital.

73. Julien and a doctor discuss the fact that Julien is hearing
strange voices in his head. The doctor tells him that it sounds
as if he is entering the early stages of schizophrenia.

74. Julien tells the doctor that his younger brother is a male
anorexic.

75. We see an image of Julien's brother screaming naked inside
a bathtub with bubbles. Julien in voice-over: 'He was scared to

take baths because he thought the water would make him fat.
My father would splash him with water and he would freak.'

76. Julien's brother is running up and down the steps in his
home. It makes a thump with every step taken. Julien in voice-
over: 'He would run up and down the stairs 400 times a day in
order to lose weight. My dad would have to recarpet the steps.'

77. Julien's brother sitting on the toilet. He is cutting the top
part of his forearm. Blood drips out the thin slice. There are
many small scars opening the open cut. Julien in voice-over:
'When he cut himself the blood made him smile.'

78. Julien watches his sister do ballet.

79. In the hospital, one of the patients has pins in her legs. She
is very old. She looks straight into Julien's eyes. Julien says,
'Hey, Bobby, how is your leg holding up?' She responds, 'Hi yo
silverware, Tonto's lost his underwear! What the heck do I care?'

80. Gay patient sits by himself in his room staring sadly at a
picture of the boy he once loved.

81. Julien is standing in his room painting himself in blackface.
He is only wearing tight white underwear; the rest of his body
is covered in black paint. He picks up a broken banjo and
dances a little jig. Julien in voice-over: 'I had always wanted to
be black. I can't have soul if I ain't black. Sammy Davis Jr.,
M.C. Hammer, Marvin Gaye. Someone once told me that if a
black guy gets a tan he'll turn purple. I love purple.' He jumps
in the air and spins.

82. Julien's sister is speaking on the telephone to the boy that
got her pregnant. He tells her he wants nothing to do with the
child. She hangs up.

83. Julien reads a poem he wrote to his family as they sit in
front of the dinner table.

84. They all eat a big turkey.

85. In the hospital hallway we see an eight-foot man with a slight hunchback doing karate.

86. Julien is making another newsletter out of red cardboard paper.

87. Julien says hello to a forty-year-old senile man, who grabs his shirt collar and screams, 'It's time for my abortion, Julien. I'm already in my third trimester. I can tell the baby is starting to kick.'

88. A woman falls out of her wheelchair, screaming, 'Lord? Lord?'

89. We see a quick montage of other people attached to machines.

90. Julien is showering another group of patients with a shiny hose.

91. The hospital is in a lonely cul-de-sac, with an almost empty view of trees.

92. Spring. Various flowers and leaves.

93. Julien is at a formal dance in his hospital auditorium.

94. At the end of the dance one of the patients, an old black man in a three-piece suit and long white tap shoes, is lying dead, stuck in between the closing elevator doors; he suffered a stroke. A small crowd of patients dressed in their formal wear are all standing quietly. They are watching the doors go back and forth on the dead man's body; each time the doors try to close the dead man gets picked up for a moment and then flops back. His hairpiece is coming undone. The eight-foot-tall man bends down and picks up the dead black guy and drapes

him over his shoulder in one mighty swoop. He walks down the hallway as the crowd continues to watch. A few of the senile patients begin to clap and cheer.

95. In the hospital auditorium, a Baptist church is putting on a Bible pageant. A skinny forty-five-year-old magician with a nervous eye twitch is on stage entertaining everyone.

96. Julien is in the audience holding hands with a female who stands about 4'4" tall. She is wearing an Indian head-dress and cowboy gloves. She has a pleasantly round face and is missing two bottom lower teeth.

97. The skinny magician looks out at the audience and says, 'I can die and resurrect myself. I can fly. I can drown myself. I can light myself on fire. Disappear. Walk on water. Twist my head completely around. Melt myself. ESP. Break my leg and then fix it back. Put my finger all the way inside my ear. Slide upside down on my head. Walk through walls. Eat light bulbs and cement. Take twenty punches in the face. Just about anything.'

98. Julien is sucking on the girl's chin. She is awestruck by the skinny magician.

99. The skinny magician sticks four packs of cigarettes in his mouth all at once. He lights them with a small torch. He takes a few puffs, then swallows the whole thing completely. He has a huge grin on his face as smoke rings start coming out of his ears. The audience gives him a standing ovation. The magician bows and then quickly darts off stage.

100. Julien and the 4'4"-tall woman are waiting for the bus. A dog walks by, and Julien begins to bark at it as loud as he can.

101. Julien and the short woman are making love on the floor inside her small living room. She has a tiny infant baby that is sleeping, tucked away in a bundle of blankets on the sofa a few

feet away from their lovemaking. Julien has to always have the
TV on in order to have sex. Julien keeps popping his head up
to stare at the sleeping child.

102. The next morning. TVs and garden sprinklers make
noises outside. Cars go by.

103. Julien is washing the short woman's feet with a scrub
brush and a yellow plastic bowl of warm water. She dips both
feet in the bowl and says, 'I loved the way your testicles felt last
night. I love their weight and symmetry.' Julien doesn't really
understand her. He looks up at her in disgust.

104. She gives a long speech about how all her boyfriends have
all had tragically short lives, violence and strange diseases
mainly. As she tells the story, I will show the dead boyfriends
with a series of still photos. Maria Callas sings underneath.

105. We see the short woman working for an airline, checking
in passengers. She is standing on a wooden box.

106. Outside in the windy clarity, children splash around the
apartment complex's tiny pool.

107. The scene from the beginning repeats again – an old moving image of a beautiful woman in a swim cap calmly holding a
beach ball as the waves curl over her back. Julien in voice-over:
'My mother, my mother. She was so pretty. My mother, my
mother, they lopped off her tittie. My mother had hair like a
gold Olympic medal. She lost it to the Russians and got a
bronze. Her high jump was best though. I still think she saw
Jesus in a shoe and that's where she is.'

108. Julien's little brother looks for a job. He tries to become a
lifeguard but tells the employer that he will not go in after anyone if they are drowning, but that he can blow the loudest
whistle to get everyone's attention.

109. Julien crying in the bathtub. He is wearing red lipstick. He gives an extremely deadpan monologue to no one at all: 'A mother abuses her son sexually. I started having fantasies about him when he was very young. I miss you more than Jackson Mississippi (misses-sipi). I knew a guy who was an art lover. He had two daughters. He named one Mona and the other Lisa. A girl sits in a room bored to death. She starts to cry. She decides life isn't worth living. She pulls out a dull knife and tries to slit her wrist. Nothing cuts. She cries out, "I'm such a failure!" A man falls in love with a girl. But he can't have her. He films her in the garden. The man projects her image against the wall. He kisses her face as it's being projected. I saw a three-year-old child on the TV pick out the country of Macedonia off a flat map. Every man has his tales of woe. Unfortunately in life there's more woe than tale. My son was killed. When I went to the dentist I started to freak out and cry because I remembered taking Jimmie there to get his braces fixed. And I remembered how he looked in his braces.' Julien starts smacking his face hard, this time on his own jaw, cheeks, forehead, lips, etc. A little bit of blood drips from his nose and lips and drops into the white soapy water.

110. It's magic hour and the wind is blowing steady outside. We see a picture of the murdered little turtle boy. It is a photo xerox copy of his face smiling. Under his face in large letters it says, 'Missing boy. 1,000$ reward.' The flyers are strapped and pasted to every telephone pole and mailbox that the eye can see, for blocks upon blocks. The wind makes the flyers flap loudly like speeding drums. Some of the pictures of the boy's face are tearing apart and worn down.

111. Julien is standing in his underwear in the bathroom. He is taking pills that the doctor prescribed to him in order to help the voices subside. He has a difficult time undoing the lid.

112. Julien and his sister are in the basement together laughing. Julien has his ear on her belly listening for any sound. She lets him rub her belly gently with the palm of her hand. She relaxes

and closes her eyes. He continues rubbing his sister's tummy.
He looks at her resting peacefully with her head propped up on
a big yellow pillow. With the other hand Julien begins to rub
her thighs up and down. He stares at her face lovingly. She
opens her eyes and tells him that one day he'll make a fine
daddy. Julien says nothing, just continues to rub her. She rubs
his cheeks and tells him how for the first time she will have
created something all her own, a baby to take care of and love.
Julien doesn't seem all that interested in what she has to say.
He just continues sitting there like a robot, rubbing his pregnant sister's thighs and belly.

113. Back at the hospital. In one room a man with blue skin is
cutting his toenails.

114. In another room sit a man and a wife who no longer
remember each other's names.

115. Julien and his younger brother and father go back to
church and sing in the choir. The black minister is wearing a
neckbrace and a Bruce Springsteen button on his navy blue
dress jacket. At one point in the service the minister sneezes
fourteen times in a row and after every sneeze the congregation yells out, 'Bless you. Bless you, Jesus!!!'

116. Afterwards the three of them stand in front of the church
and watch all the people drive away in their cars and buses.

117. Julien is in his room doing sit-ups and pull-ups.

118. He stares at himself in a full-length mirror and sticks the
rifle at his head. Looking at himself in the mirror with his gun
he says, 'I had always loved the world. I loved pickles. I loved
horses. I loved the Lord. I loved the tin cans that Peter and
Poncho and the other kids would throw at my head when I was
little. Once I saw a naked couple sitting around in an abandoned car. I loved to watch. It's just that sometimes I feel disoriented . . . Then I saw Hitler. I saw the skinny Jewish people.

I could feel my belly rot. Those Jews were slaughtered like chickens. My father said, "I should die like the Jews." He said I could get a free tattoo in heaven. I saw him grab Lumpy bunny by the neck and he says bunnies grow up on clouds up there with them Jews. But my heart was full of love. It's OK to die, he said. Look at all the skinny dead Jews. He said the world circles no matter what.'

119. Julien drops the gun to the floor and begins making muscles and posing in the mirror. He continues to speak: 'I have no muscles, only skin and bones. Marilyn Monroe had six toes on her left foot.'

120. Julien is in the kitchen making his younger brother bark like a dog. Julien keeps slapping his brother's face with long thin straps of wet bacon. Julien starts kicking his brother's face into the cabinet.

121. Julien is resting his head under the tire of a parked truck at the local gas station. When the owner of the car walks up and asks Julien what he's doing with his head under his tire, Julien answers that he wanted a good rest but there aren't any pillows left at the house.

122. Julien asleep by himself inside White Castle hamburger restaurant. It's 4.00 a.m.

123. Julien and his sister are playing music inside her bedroom. She plays the cello and he sings made-up words in a deep operatic style.

124. His father threatens to break his sister's cello. Julien argues back and his father makes him punch his face over and over again till Julien busts open his own lip. But Julien just smiles and keeps it up harder and harder, hitting himself while he stares his dad down. Julien's face is covered in blood. Julien's sister is yelling and begging Julien to quit hitting himself. Julien just smiles.

125. Julien, his sister, and his blind girlfriend are all three at an ice-skating rink. Julien is sitting next to a ten-year-old Hassidic Jewish boy. They are both eating large scoops of strawberry ice cream. The Hassidic boy is very cute with puffy cheeks and he is wearing all of the required formal religious uniform. They both have ice skates on, except that Julien is wearing a pair of ice skates that he made out of cheap plastic flip-flops with his bare toes exposed. He explains his invention of flip-flop ice skates to the Hassidic boy and offers to sell them at a discount price. The Hassidic boy looks pissed off at Julien's ridiculous invention, and then proceeds to curse Julien out in Yiddish.

126. Julien's sister and girlfriend are sitting next to each other lacing up their skates. Julien's sister is closely observing the blind girl. She seems transfixed by her every movement and gesture. Julien's sister says, 'The world is too loud. I wish I was deaf. I have always tried to pop my ear drums. Sometimes I'll stick a Q-tip too far inside my ear. I don't want to hear any more. I only want to see. To see without hearing.'

127. The two girls are ice skating around the rink next to one another. People everywhere are watching how amazingly the blind girl skates. She gracefully spins, jumps, twirls, and twists without fault.

128. Julien and the Hassidic boy are silently watching the two girls.

129. Julien's sister is skating slowly on the ice. She begins to smile in amazement at the blind girl's beauty and grace, but while watching the girl she stops paying attention to her own poor on-ice ability and all of a sudden gets her skates tangled up together. She slips forward and falls down hard onto her pregnant belly.

130. Julien is the first to notice and he screams out, 'Fire!!! My sister's on fire!!!'

131. Julien's sister starts screaming out in pain and agony. She is squirming like a fish out of water and starts screaming for Julien as loud as she can. She is on the ice holding her belly. Julien runs onto the ice and slides up next to her and begins to hold her like a baby. Everyone else in the arena quickly converges around Julien's fallen sister.

132. The ten-year-old Hassidic Jewish boy stands up alone in the bleachers. He begins to sing a beautiful Hebrew prayer song. Then he sits back down and continues to finish licking his strawberry ice-cream cone.

133. The only person not circled around Julien's sister is Julien's blind girlfriend, who is totally oblivious to all that is going on around her. She begins skating faster and more beautifully than ever before, almost as if she were competing in the Olympics. As she twirls and spins around the ice, we hear the horrible screams of pain that are emanating from Julien's fallen sister.

Added Scenes

1. Julien tries to coach his brother in wrestling. He asks his sister for a pair of her underwear and bra. She asks why, and he explains that all the best wrestlers wear costumes. So he puts on a pair of her leopard-skin underwear and a black silk bra. He pulls his nylon black socks all the way up to his knees and then puts a gas mask over his face. He makes up a wrestling name for himself, calling himself 'Julien the Jamming Jabber.' His sister is the referee. She announces both her brothers, who are standing on opposite sides of the living room. Their father is sitting on the couch silently enjoying the spectacle. He is eating a banana and one half of his moustache is shaved off, leaving the other side fully grown. The two of them fight around on the floor in a half-way serious battle. Julien's sister is skipping around the room clapping her hands and in a consciously altered deep voice narrates the action. Father turns the radio onto a classical-music station. The music is somber and is in contrast to the excitement of the wrestling match. All of a sud-

den Julien just starts hugging his younger brother. His younger brother pushes him away and tries to get Julien angry enough to continue. Julien just jumps back on him and continues to sustain a tight-gripped bear hug. He begins kissing his little brother on the side of his cheek over and over again. Julien's little brother throws Julien down hard onto the floor and begins to violently curse him for not taking the wrestling match seriously. Julien just starts saying, 'I love you, brother,' over and over again without pause, a hundred times. Julien's little brother runs over and kicks Julien in the face. Then he runs out the front door of the house. Julien continues his one-line rant without hesitation or pause. Julien's father, now finished eating his banana, throws the peel onto the carpeted floor and says, 'Disqualified for bad behavior.'

2. Julien is standing on a somewhat busy sidewalk, he is pacing quickly from one side to the other. He goes up to the passing strangers and tries to explain to them that he is the reincarnation of Moses. He also tells people elementary-school jokes and then asks them if he thinks they sound funny. He laughs after every joke he tells in a very annoying fake laugh.

3. Julien tells one of the blind people that he is saving up all his money to buy the holy grail.

4. Julien loves to say, 'Jesus has a penis.'

5. Julien whistles to some of the blind patients.

6. Julien tape-records his father snoring and plays it for some of the blind patients. He laughs at it like it's the funniest thing in the world.

7. Julien counts all the notable points on his sister's naked body. He takes a magic marker and plays connect the dots with the moles on her back. She enjoys it and lets him do it willingly.

julien donkey-boy: Ewen Bremner as Julien.

CAST AND CREW

MAIN CAST

JULIEN	Ewen Bremner
PEARL	Chloë Sevigny
JULIEN'S FATHER	Werner Herzog
CHRIS	Evan Neumann
GRANDMA	Joyce Korine
CHRISSY	Chrissy Kobylak
RAPPER	Victor Varnado
GYNECOLOGIST	Virginia Reath
CARD-PLAYING NEIGHBOR	Alvin Law
MAGICIAN	Tom Mullica
HASSIDIC BOY	Ricky Ashley
NURSE	Carmela García

MAIN CREW

Directed by	Harmony Korine
Written by	Harmony Korine
Produced by	Scott Macaulay
	Robin O'Hara
	Cary Woods
Line producer	Jim Czarnecki
Cinematography by	Anthony Dod Mantle
Film Editing by	Valdis Óskarsdóttir
Casting by	Kerry Barden
	Lori Eastside
	Billy Hopkins
	Suzanne Smith

Slow motion: a girl figure skating. Opera plays in the background.
She spins and jumps.

CUT TO:

EXT. A FIELD — DAY

Julien wanders in a snowy field, looking around. He is young,
maybe in his twenties, but acts and looks like he's younger. He seems
lost.

He approaches a small boy off-camera.

> JULIEN
> All right. Whatcha got?

> BOY
> A turtle.

Julien looks concerned, confused.

> JULIEN
> Whoa . . . oh, man. What're you gonna do with it?

He wanders after the boy. A pause.

> You wanna play turtle with me?

> BOY
> If you can find another one, I think there's another one in
> there.

Julien picks up and examines the turtle, laughing, smiling.

> JULIEN
> (*still laughing*)
> Whoa . . . is there twelve turtles in the pond?

He keeps laughing.

There's eleven turtles in this pond, and . . . two turtles on the rock . . .

Boy looks around, listening.

Yeah, I got a turtle . . . Where're the turtles, huh? Where're the turtles?

Julien grabs handfuls of mud, staggers a little.

You didn't get nothing for daddy?

BOY
No, you can't get one.

Very quickly, Julien grabs the boy and forces him into the mud, smothering him; we view the struggle from the boy's POV. The struggle stops and Julien looks down, confused, upset.

JULIEN
Almighty God, see now your son as he lies in great weakness . . . and bless him with everlasting life.

Now we are in voice-over as Julien buries the boy.

In the name, your son, have mercy on him, lamb of God, take away our sins, have mercy on him, take away our sins . . .

Julien repeats this as he continues covering the boy in dirt.

CUT TO:

EXT. DUSK

We follow Julien in a blur as he moves down the street. The trees are bare; he is in a daze. Spare guitar plays in the background.

CUT TO:

EXT. STREET – NIGHT

A blur of cars, lights, street sounds. We come to Julien's house.

CUT TO:

INT. PEARL'S BEDROOM – NIGHT

A blonde pregnant ballerina, Julien's sister Pearl, dances to classical music.

    CUT TO:

INT. FATHER'S BEDROOM – NIGHT

Julien's father is dancing, too. He drinks cough syrup, spinning slowly.

    CUT TO:

INT. LIVING ROOM – NIGHT

Grandmother holds a little white dog over her head on the couch.

                    GRANDMOTHER
Kiss kiss. Kiss Mommy, kiss Mommy. I love Punky . . .
he's a nice baby.

    CUT TO:

INT. STAIRCASE – NIGHT

Julien's brother crawls up the stairs, then runs back down.

    CUT TO:

INT. PEARL'S BEDROOM – NIGHT

Pearl dances in front of a mirror.

    CUT TO:

INT. FATHER'S BEDROOM – NIGHT

Julien's father is still dancing, spinning.

    CUT TO:

INT. PEARL'S BEDROOM – NIGHT

Pearl spins slowly in her room. The music is quieter.

CUT TO:

INT. LIVING ROOM — NIGHT

We return to grandmother with dog.

> **GRANDMOTHER**
> I love Punky, Mommy say, 'Punky nice baby.' You love Mommy?

CUT TO:

INT. FATHER'S BEDROOM — NIGHT

Julien's father dances, dances.

CUT TO:

INT. STAIRCASE — NIGHT

Julien watches from the stairs as Pearl dances. We jump to a close-up as he studies her.

CUT TO:

INT. PEARL'S BEDROOM — NIGHT

Short series of stills of Pearl in her outfit.

CUT TO:

INT. BATHROOM — DAY

Julien sits in the bathtub, wet, a look of concentration on his face.

Jump cut as he prays, mumbles, slaps himself, prays again. He splashes in the bath.

> **JULIEN**
> Hail Lord Julien, hail Lord Julien . . . Julien Lord! Julien Lord!

CUT TO:

INT. BATHROOM — DAY

Close-up of Julien, still in the tub, singing 'Frère Jacques' with different words, eyes closed.

>   JULIEN
> Frer-e-jak-a, Frer-e-jak-a, Mommy too, Mommy too,
> ding-a-long-a-lula, ding-a-longa-lula, I love you, I'll be
> you . . .

>   CUT TO:

INT. BATHROOM — DAY

Medium shot: Julien still singing in the tub.

>   JULIEN
> Frer-er-jak-a, Frer-er-jak, Mommy too, Mommy too,
> where are all the monkeys, where are all the monkeys, in
> the zoo . . .

>   CUT TO:

INT. BATHROOM — DAY

Julien standing, naked, looking out the window, still in the bath. He gyrates, singing, repeating the same line over and over.

>   JULIEN
> That's what I wanna know, that's what I wanna know . . .

>   CUT TO:

INT. DINING ROOM — DAY

Julien sits at the dinner table with his family, next to his brother Chris. Julien laughs.

>   CHRIS
> Take your teeth out.

Julien removes his false teeth.

                                JULIEN
   Sorry, Chris.

Family members talk about Julien's teeth.

   Chris got me these for my birthday.

                                CHRIS
   They're nice, right?

                                JULIEN
   They're excellent.

Julien rinses his teeth in his glass of Kool-Aid.

   I only rinse 'em on Tuesdays.

                                FATHER
   C'mon, this looks like a steak dinner when the Queen was
   Russia and there was this president and his name is
   Brezhnev and he had these false teeth and during the
   steak dinner he would take out his false teeth and clean it
   with a fork.

Pearl makes a face of disgust.

                                PEARL
   After he . . . After he ate?

                             JULIEN (O.S.)
   I gotta do that as well.

Family discusses Pearl's posture.

                                FATHER
   Tell her to sit straight.

Grandmother looks over at Pearl.

                            GRANDMOTHER
   Yeah, how you eat?

Father is insistent.

                                FATHER
   No, she should sit straight.

GRANDMOTHER

Yeah, OK, has she?

(*turning to Pearl*)

How you eat? You eat good? You like it?

PEARL

Yeah.

Grandmother keeps rambling about the food. Father looks at his daughter, then speaks to grandmother.

FATHER

She should sit straight. Tell her to sit straight, Pearl, she listens to you.

Pearl sits straight; we see her pregnant belly.

PEARL

Jeez.

JULIEN

Papa, why's she sit straight?

FATHER

Forget her, look at your brother.

Chris looks around nervously.

He thinks he's a wrestler. Look at the guy. Doesn't make sense to me.

CUT TO:

INT. FATHER'S BEDROOM – DAY

Father is sitting on a bed, naked except for a pair of boxer shorts and a gas mask. He is reading the back of a bottle.

FATHER

'Do not take Prolact if you are hypersensitive.'

CUT TO:

Father near window, looking at bottle, now without the gas mask.

                              FATHER
Hypersensitive.

He takes a swig.

    Am I hypersensitive?

*Jump cut to father pouring the syrup into his slipper. He tries to
drink it, but it spills everywhere.*

    Oh my God . . .

Another jump to father spinning his arm, talking to himself.

    Am I hypersensitive? Am I persistent?

He drinks more, looks at the bottle.

    Natural high. Like in the mountains. High up.

Father takes another swig.

    Where are you Mount Everest? Give me some Everest.

    CUT TO:

EXT. STREET — DAY

*Slow dissolve from Julien and father walking down the street to a
close-up of Julien's father's face. We hear father speaking in voice-
over.*

                         FATHER (V.O.)
I started something like this in the aftermath of the . . .
Spanish Conquest of Peru. There was a lot of infighting,
you know, they formed parties and there was this un-
believable amount of greed among the Spanish and there
was on the one side Pissarro and his brothers and on the
other there was El Magro and he was one of the principle
leaders and, boy, the guy really looked so ugly they sent a
delegation to the Spanish king and El Magro looked so
gross and so ugly they couldn't even send him out there,
and there's this wonderful story about this old Spanish
nobleman who was well into his seventies who's been

involved in campaigns back in Europe and then the conquest of Mexico, conquest of Peru, he was white-haired
and in all this fighting, he was on one side, I think sticking
to Pissarro's side, and all of the sudden he rides into an
ambush of his enemies and he rides on his horse and they
point their muskets at him and they are just about to
shoot him and he knows that he's going to be dead in a
minute and he just defiantly sings a song against them,
and what he sings is 'Little Mother, Two by Two Wasps,
the Wind on My Hair.' I truly like that.

CUT TO:

EXT. STREET — DAY

*Julien walks through the streets, headphones playing music, his eyes
closed.*

CUT TO:

INT. HOME FOR THE BLIND — DAY

A series of still frames; Julien hugs a large woman.

WOMAN

What're you doing?

Julien holds her, mumbling.

CUT TO:

INT. HOME FOR THE BLIND — DAY

*Another set of stills; Julien looks out the window with a Hispanic
man wearing sunglasses.*

JULIEN

Come here, come here, come here. See from here, I can
see all the way, I can see all the way across from New York
City almost all the way across to Los Angeles.

MAN

Oh, man! The big time, baby!

JULIEN

I can see all the way from here to the other side of America.

MAN

Whoa!

JULIEN

All the way over to the West Coast. I can see right over from the East Coast to the West Coast.

MAN

Oh, man, oh, man. Thanks, man, for telling me, man, damn.

CUT TO:

INT. HOME FOR THE BLIND – DAY

Another set; Julien and a young man work at fixing a copier. The young man is also wearing sunglasses. Both these men are blind.

YOUNG MAN

There's no paper in this thing.

JULIEN

No, you got paper, it's in the plastic box.

YOUNG MAN

You're right, you're right.

JULIEN

It's full, it's full. That sounds like it's moving.

YOUNG MAN

I'm trying to make it move. It's doing nothing . . . I think we need that guy from the office.

CUT TO:

INT. HOME FOR THE BLIND – DAY

Another set of stills; Julien in the bathroom with a boy. It is unclear what has taken place; the boy looks down, Julien washes his hands.

> JULIEN

You better wash your hands.

CUT TO:

INT. HOME FOR THE BLIND — DAY

Another set; Julien wrests a trash can away from a retarded boy; they embrace.

CUT TO:

INT. HOME FOR THE BLIND — DAY

Another set; we hear people bowling. Julien is gathering bowling shoes. A boy prepares to bowl.

> BOY

I ain't wearing no shoes, let me tell you. Look.

> JULIEN

What size?

> BOY

Uh, seven.

Julien retrieves the shoes.

CUT TO:

INT. BOWLING ALLEY — DAY

Now we are back to moving frames. A young Asian boy in a wheel-chair cheers his ball as it moves down the lane.

> ASIAN BOY

Go, go, go!

It knocks down some pins; everyone cheers.

A small blind girl, Christie, prepares to bowl. Julien goes to get her another ball.

JULIEN

You want that? You got a heavy one. This one's lighter,
this one's lighter.

*She bowls; everyone cheers. She bowls again. A few pins are knocked
down.*

After Christie finishes, she seems upset. Julien tries to help.

A tall black kid bowls a gutterball with a huge swing.

Another blind kid bowls.

JULIEN (O.S.)

Get back from the line, man, get back from the line.

The blind kid turns and laughs.

You cheated, you cheated already.

*More bowling. The blind kid returns to bowl, checks his feet at the
line. He bowls; people cheer.*

Julien bowls a strike.

CUT TO:

EXT. ALLEY — DAY

*Outside it's a gray, grimy day. Julien's father is hosing off Chris in
an alley behind their house. Chris cowers from the water, obviously
cold, wearing nothing but a pair of trunks.*

FATHER

This is it. Don't scream, I don't want you to scream. This
is it.

We get closer.

Come on, keep still.

CHRIS

Stop!

FATHER

Don't shift around. Come on, be a man. Be a man and

quit that move-y groovy. Quit that.

CHRIS

It's too cold!

FATHER

Come over here.

CHRIS

Stop! Stop it! Dad!

FATHER

Come on, be a man! It might even seep through your skin and you put on some weight.

CHRIS

Shut up!

FATHER

Come on, you don't talk like this.

CHRIS

Shut up!

FATHER

You don't talk like this! Just be a man. Come on, go down here. Go down, squat down. OK, come here, come here, I don't want this escaping . . . just, all this move-y groovy, I just don't like that. Down, down, raise your arm! Come on, come closer to me and don't be a coward, I don't want a coward in the family. Come here!

CHRIS

You want me to win? You want me to win?

FATHER

Yes, I want you to win! Don't be a coward. My son is not gonna be a coward.

CHRIS

Stop it! Stop.

FATHER

Dad is gonna put some wet on you! Stop that shivering, I

don't want you to shiver like that, don't shiver!

Chris shivers.

You're a man. OK? Don't shiver like that. You're gonna be a winner, just don't shiver. A winner doesn't shiver.

CUT TO:

INT. STAIRCASE — DAY

Chris crawls up the stairs using only his hands. It's hard work and he's visibly tired. When he gets to the top, he runs back down and starts up on his hands again.

CUT TO:

INT. CHRIS'S ROOM — DAY

A set of stills. Chris with a knife. He puts the knife to his throat, his eyes blacked out. We hear him in voice-over.

CHRIS (V.O.)
Fuck. Can't ever fuckin' win, gonna be a winner, gonna fuckin' be a winner, you're not a fuckin' loser.

CUT TO:

EXT. FIELD — DAY

Pearl walks through a wheat field. The light is golden and the sun behind her gives the appearance of a halo. She sings.

PEARL
Oh, God, you take away the sins of the world/Have mercy on us/Oh, God, you take away the sins of the world/Have mercy on us/Oh, God, you take away the sins of the world/Grant us peace/Lean on Jesus/Lean on Jesus/Lean on the everlasting Love/La la la la la/Lean on the everlasting Love.

CUT TO:

INT. THRIFT STORE – DAY

Pearl is in a seedy thrift store, looking through baby clothes.

> PEARL
> That's cute . . . that's too dirty.

She goes to the counter, talking to the clerk.

> How much are the onesies?

> CLERK
> Two for a dollar.

> PEARL
> Two for a dollar? I'm looking for more newborn stuff.

> CLERK
> Did you look on the table?

> PEARL
> On the table they're . . . bigger, there's no really, no really infant clothes on the table, it's mostly in the boxes, and I don't know what I'm gonna have so I have to get, you know, both, both . . . I think it might be a boy, though.

> CLERK
> First one?

> PEARL
> I think it might be a boy because . . .

> CLERK
> First one?

> PEARL
> Yeah, 'cause I might have seen . . .

> CLERK
> You blessed . . . you blessed then . . .

> PEARL
> I might have, I might have seen a teeny weenie on the sonogram.

CLERK

Yeah, well you, that mean you blessed.

MAN AT COUNTER

That's your first child?

CLERK

First baby.

PEARL

It's my first baby.

CLERK

They say you blessed, your womb is blessed when you have a boy first, I don't know . . .

PEARL

Oh really?

CLERK

Yeah . . .

PEARL

That's kind of sexist, don't you think?

CLERK

I don't know. They say first a boy and second a girl. The girls come in after a boy, you know that . . . You have twenty-five cents?

PEARL

I don't, I don't, I'm sorry.

CLERK

Here you go, good luck.

PEARL

Thank you.

MAN AT COUNTER

Good luck.

PEARL

Thank you.

Pearl walks out, holds the door for a man in a wheelchair.

CUT TO:

INT. DOCTOR'S OFFICE – DAY

Pearl's hands over her pregnant belly. She is being examined by a female doctor.

OB-GYN

So now I'm gonna do an internal on you, OK?

PEARL

OK.

OB-GYN

And you're just gonna feel some jelly, OK? It's a little cold, all right? Let's try to relax, you're gonna feel my fingers, OK? You all right?

PEARL

Mm-hm.

OB-GYN

OK, everything feels good, getting big. OK, head's down . . . OK . . . good. Put your legs together . . . So who's the father?

CUT TO:

INT. JULIEN'S HOUSE – DAY

A series of blurred stills, music. Julien and Pearl dancing, Julien smiling, Pearl smiling. They are cheek to cheek.

CUT TO:

EXT. STREET – DAY

Julien stands on a street corner, talking to himself, wearing his headphones. People walk by; he sometimes engages them.

JULIEN

Why, why is the wind blind? The wind's actually blind.

'Cause, um, wind's a breeze, breeze's a zephyr, zephyr's
yours . . . I can't get over it, I can't get over it, I can't get
over it, I can't, I cannot get over it, I can't get over it, you
know what I mean? Hers as well, I like hers as well . . .
NYPD, LAPD, NYPD, LAPD . . . all right, all right,
you're my friend, you're my friend . . . where's my
brother?

He looks at passing cars.

If you make the hill go downhill, it's gonna be a lot easier
. . . this part is too . . . so make it go downhill, it's gonna
be much easier, the hill's going up, look how quickly the
hill goes up, you get a hill that goes downhill, it's gonna be
much, much easier . . . all the way to Santa Fe, yeah yeah
yeah yeah . . .

Julien goes toward a family passing by.

Excuse me excuse me excuse me excuse me, do you know
my family tree, is my family tree this tree or that tree . . .

WOMAN
I don't know.

JULIEN
I've a family in my tree, and my family, and I've got one . . .
to the other tree, or to the other tree? It's hard to tell, hard
to tell, hard to tell, hard to tell . . . wherever you are, wherever you are . . . NYPD, LAPD, NYPD, LAPD . . . you
know me, all right . . . you're a friend of my brother . . .

CUT TO:

INT. CHURCH — DAY

*Red candles flickering in a church. In the back we can see an image
of Jesus; the candles begin to blur. A sermon echoes.*

CUT TO:

INT. CHURCH — DAY

Julien is in a confessional, we see his POV as he stares at the grate separating the priest and himself.

JULIEN

God is looking on me. With, um, his ghost. Jesus has been seeing me. He thinks that I should not be a member of the church community any longer and . . . I just feel very diffi-cult.

PRIEST

But those sentiments aren't from God, nor from Christ, and . . . it flies in the face of all that we've been taught about God and the ministry of God and Jesus and . . . the holy Father is compassionate and his reign falls upon the just and the unjust as sun shines upon the good and the wicked, because that's how he is, God is good, and God is love, and there's no room in God for looking upon a child of his with disgust or want to cast him off from the body of Christ or something like that . . . so, um, these are thoughts that we can impose on ourselves or, or actually the power of darkness can as it were whisper them in our ear, but I really have to say to you that they're not from God. Have you ever done counseling with anybody, or, uh, therapy with anybody . . . psychotherapy, I mean?

JULIEN

Oh, yeah, I know what you mean. No, I haven't.

PRIEST

We have a counseling center here, if I could give you that there, right.

Priest hands Julien a pamphlet.

I give that to you just because there are names and phone numbers there, right? And they could be helpful for a phone conversation, um, or just to kind of come in one time and have a talk, you know, this kind of thing. But there's no reason for a young man like yourself to, um, to

think that, you know, either being anxious or stressful is
an untreatable situation.

JULIEN

Thank you very much.

PRIEST

All right. I'll give you a blessing anyway before you go. All
right?

JULIEN

Thank you. Thank you very much.

Julien exits the confessional.

CUT TO:

INT. HOTEL ROOM — DAY

A nun masturbates on the floor of a hotel room, slaps herself.

Julien's voice can be overheard in voice-over.

JULIEN (V.O.)

Sometimes I have sinful thoughts.

CUT TO:

INT. CHURCH — DAY

Moving down a hallway; at the end there is an icon of the Virgin.

CUT TO:

INT. LIVING ROOM — DAY

*Julien's father is doing card tricks with an armless man. He wears a
watch on his ankle and uses his feet like hands.*

They are in the living room. Figure skating plays on TV.

ARMLESS MAN

My mom told me when I was six years old that all I have
to do was grab the energy. I don't have the strength, I
don't have the body, you have to have the energy.

Julien's father shuffles the cards. He is dismissive.

> FATHER
>
> It's a mistake, and that's it.

> ARMLESS MAN
>
> No, that's not it, it's energy.

> FATHER
>
> Look at her.

Father motions towards the figure skater on TV.

> ARMLESS MAN
>
> See, she's got the energy.

> FATHER
>
> Yeah, yeah, yeah, but it's backwards. It's . . . is it a triple axel?

> ARMLESS MAN
>
> I don't know what it is. Who cares what it is? Look at her do that, see?

A blurry view of the figure skater, the same one as in the opening. Opera plays as she performs her routine.

The armless man's foot takes a card from the top of the deck.

> FATHER
>
> It's not going to be an ace.

> ARMLESS MAN
>
> Wanna bet? There it is again.

> FATHER
>
> The hell with . . . you're cheating, you're cheating all the time.

> ARMLESS MAN
>
> What?

> FATHER
>
> You're just cheating all the time.

ARMLESS MAN

What? Cards up my *sleeve*? I don't think so.

FATHER

Yeah, but you are hiding the aces somewhere, I wouldn't
say up your sleeves, but . . .

ARMLESS MAN

No. See, no sleeves.

Armless man lifts up his legs to show the obvious.

See, no sleeves.

FATHER

Yeah, but the aces are there, yeah, it's true, no?

ARMLESS MAN

No, I tell ya what, it's as simple as that, when you're born
different, stuff happens, some stuff's good, some stuff's
bad . . . for me, it worked out.

Father sets down the deck on the coffee table again.

FATHER

It won't be an ace again. It won't be an ace again.

ARMLESS MAN

You don't wanna bet any money on this?

Armless man takes off the top card again with his foot. It's an ace.

There it is again.

FATHER

They're really not shuffled.

ARMLESS MAN

Anything's possible, it's magic, these . . . magic toes. She's
got magic toes too, but hers are in skates.

Another blurry figure skater.

FATHER

How do you do that?

ARMLESS MAN

I told you, I learned it as a kid. It was my equalizer,
you're born without arms, you learn to use your feet,
that's the physical part. The rest, that's where you learn,
it's where . . . it's the attitude, look, she's got attitude too.
You come over here and thought about your world, and
I'm telling you, you just have to adopt a positive attitude.
It's not like those people on TV that sell you stuff, it's
real life! It's like the ace, it keeps coming up, we're not on
TV . . .

Father slams down the deck again.

. . . we're real life.

FATHER

Grab it! Grab it! Grab it!

ARMLESS MAN

Top card again? You want the top card again?

Armless man grabs the card. It's an ace again.

It could be anyone, see? It could be in the middle, it could
be anywhere, it's on top, there it is again. Attitude. Positive
thinking. I know, it sounds like crap, but it works for me.
Here, cheers . . .

They tap their tea mugs together. Armless man drinks with his foot.

You're my friend. I don't do it to hurt ya, I do it to show
you a lesson, to help you learn, buddy.

CUT TO:

EXT. JULIEN'S HOUSE – DAY

*Outside, looking at a window in Julien's house. The venetian blinds
go up and down, emitting a terrible noise. A figure is visible in the
window moving back and forth.*

*Now inside, the blinds are going up and down because Julien's
father has wrapped the cord controlling the blinds around his throat.*

He rocks back and forth; the blinds go up and down.

Chris approaches the room.

FATHER

Come on in, Chris.

Chris enters, quietly, eyes downcast. He sits down on the bed, next to some dresses wrapped in plastic.

Why don't you take this dress?

Chris picks up the dress, studies it.

Father comes and sits down on the other bed.

CHRIS

What do you want me to do with it?

FATHER

It belonged to your mom.

CHRIS

Yeah?

FATHER

She wore it when we got married.

Father has drawn a curly moustache on his own face.

Why don't you put it on, it's very nice. You're the only one that looks like your mother. Show me the other one, the summer dress.

Chris quickly lifts up the dress, puts it back down.

Just put it on, Chris, just put it on and dance with me.

Chris looks down at the floor.

CHRIS

. . . No.

FATHER

You see, since your mother left, I have never danced . . . I'm gonna give you ten dollars.

He takes the money from his pocket while Chris looks on.

We go outside again and look in through the window. Only Chris and the money are visible.

CHRIS

No.

FATHER

Come on, that's a lot of money.

Chris gets up and leaves.

That's as much as a guy earns in Bangladesh for a whole month. A worker in the field earns that much. It's a lot of money, a whole family lives on that. Chris, ten bucks.

We return inside, Chris leaves the room.

Father looks at the money.

CUT TO:

INT. JULIEN'S BASEMENT – DAY

Julien jumps up holding a BB gun in his basement. He is staring at the wall.

JULIEN

Hey! Catcher! Go, stay! Go! Catcher! Catcher!

Julien is talking to pictures of Hitler on his wall.

Stop movin', shut up. Listen, you're a dead man, sonny, don't ever come back, don't ever come back like in 1980 and you ate like a cancer. You killed the Jews . . . You killed the hippies, you killed all the mothers' titties, you killed fuckin' cancer, you come back in the 1980s dressed as a sheriff . . . What're you doing, what're you doing? Answer me answer me answer me answer me . . .

He throws down the gun.

Sit down, have a cup of tea, I'm only jokin'. Come on, come in, come on in. Come on, you my friend, you my friend . . .

He looks in the mirror, sees himself.

Hey, this is Julien, King Julien. How ya doin', King Julien?
Hey, my good friend, how ya doin'? Hey, this is Adolf,
Adolf . . . he ate my mother's titties . . .

Julien moves to the pictures of Hitler.

Hey, he's my friend, he's my friend, he's a good friend of
the family. He ate my mother's titties. Come in, come in
here, Adolf.

Julien moves back to the mirror.

Julien, King Julien. Yes, sir. What is it you want from me? I
want you to meet this man, a guest in your own home,
and make him feel like he can use the place, and don't
feed him to Mommy, don't feed him to Grandmother,
don't feed him to Joyce.

Julien turns away from the mirror, starts pacing around.

The promise . . . OK, so, Adolf, sit down. Now, one of the
things we wanna get clear here, at which point do you
come into the Bible, and at which point do you leave?
'Cause, in the first, in the New Testament it says that you
came into the Bible and you went off with some of the disciples at, at just before the feast of Steven, and it stated, it
stated that you took, you turned the left cheek to one of the
disciples and said, 'Never hit me on my left side, because if
you hit me on my left side, it hurts.' Anyway, that's all I
wanted to ask, anyway, while I made your acquaintance . . .

Julien returns to Hitler's picture.

I'd just like to point out a few things. Um, you oughta
come in this house, uh, you gotta you gotta you gotta you
gotta stay with me at all times, and not upset anyone else
in my family, 'cause they don't even know that I consort
with known Nazis. So, um, that's all, that's my only condi-
tion, so, be in peace.

CUT TO:

INT. PEARL'S ROOM — DAY

Pearl plays the harp.

    CUT TO:

INT. LIVING ROOM — DAY

Julien lies on the couch, covering his face with his hands.

                JULIEN
Another hard day in the jungle, another hard day at the zoo. Another hard day at the jungle, another hard day at the zoo.

    CUT TO:

INT. PEARL'S ROOM — DAY

Pearl plays 'Frère Jacques' on the harp.

    CUT TO:

EXT. JULIEN'S HOUSE — DAY

Grandmother is calling her dog, Punky. She is standing on her back porch. It's snowy, gray. Punky roots in the bushes, oblivious to her calls.

             GRANDMOTHER
Come on, here I am.

Punky keeps rooting, looking for a place to do his business.

                (*gesturing*)
Go down, go down.

He still won't come back.

You don't come? OK. Bye-bye.

She pretends to shut the door.

Punky makes his way back to the porch.

Come on, come on. Here. Come on. Punky, come on.

OK, bye-bye. Come on, come on this time.

Punky finally enters the house.

> CUT TO:

EXT. STREET — DAY

Chris is out in front of his house, dressed in his wrestling uniform.

He stretches, twists, and does handstands on the lawn.

> CUT TO:

INT. STAIRCASE — DAY

Chris is going up the stairs on his hands again, over and over.

> CUT TO:

EXT. STREET — DAY

Back out in front of the house again. Chris pins a plastic garbage can like a wrestling opponent, crushing it in the process.

He stands, puts it back where it was, pins it again.

He sits quietly, staring intently at the can. His father watches from the stoop behind him; suddenly, he pounces on the can again.

Chris picks up the can, heaves it onto the lawn. His father picks it up and walks toward Chris.

FATHER

I don't want all this plastic in my garden. And do you feel like a winner?

Father tosses the can at Chris; it lands on the sidewalk. Father comes around, sits next to Chris, holding the can.

Plastic plastic plastic plastic plastic . . .

CHRIS

I was just playing.

Father examines the can.

FATHER

Yeah, but that's not an opponent. You've gotta be tougher, real tough . . . you've gotta out-gut them, out-tough them, out-wrestle them, out . . . plastic them.

Father throws the can to the ground.

You should be a winner, there's no winner around the house.

CUT TO:

EXT. STREET — DAY

Stills of Chris and father sitting on the lawn.

CUT TO:

INT. STAIRCASE — DAY

Chris sitting at the foot of the stairs.

CHRIS

I am a winner. I AM A WINNER!

CUT TO:

INT. BEDROOM — DAY

Father sits on his bed, wearing a T-shirt, boxers, and his gas mask. Old blues plays in the background.

He smokes, talks to himself, watches a broken TV.

CUT TO:

INT. MUNICIPAL POOL — DAY

Julien and his family are at the pool. Julien wears goggles and smiles. Everyone is having fun, splashing, playing.

Julien and Pearl swim together.

CUT TO:

INT. — DAY

A grainy TV image in black and white of a figure skater. Opera plays.

CUT TO:

INT. HOUSE — NIGHT

The armless man playing the drums in a brightly lit, tacky apartment. A large black woman dances as he plays exuberantly.

> ARMLESS MAN
> That's it, yeah! I like that! Yeah!

CUT TO:

INT. HOME FOR THE BLIND — DAY

Piano plays in the background of the home where Julien works. A number of the disabled bowlers from earlier are sitting around talking.

> BLACK BLIND KID
> Um, well, see I have this problem . . . in my left eye. I don't even know what you call this vision in my left eye . . . It's not shadows, it's not anything, it's just like . . . imagine, imagine looking through a . . . um, a Food Town plastic bag, that's how my sight is, it's really weird.

> YOUNG BLIND WOMAN
> But, uh, I thank God that I'm healthy, like, uh . . . I can walk. I pray at night.

> JULIEN
> Do you ask why God did that, why God let that happen?

> YOUNG BLIND WOMAN
> Uh . . . no.

> BLACK BLIND KID
> But there's no reason why He can't fix it.

YOUNG BLIND WOMAN

No.

BLACK BLIND KID

So don't worry about it. He tells us a lot of things . . .
visions appear to blind people.

YOUNG BLIND WOMAN

God gave me intelligence.

ALBINO

Intelligence?

YOUNG BLIND WOMAN

Yeah.

ALBINO

Yeah, like, my parents, my grandparents on both sides are
ministers, and we always argue about God, 'cause I don't
really believe in church at all. 'Cause I don't, I don't nec-
essarily believe that anybody can tell you how to relate to
God, nobody can tell you, it's all up to you.

WHITE BLIND KID

Nobody can tell you how it is.

ALBINO

That's right.

WHITE BLIND KID

All he says is, 'Live just, live right' . . . all these commandments . . . live honestly, he says, yeah, he says, be honest
about who you are . . . I live day by day, I have to . . .

JULIEN

Jesus said, Jesus said, it's in the Bible, um, 'Cursed be he
who obstructs a blind man,' who, uh 'obstructs a blind
man's path,' who 'puts an obstacle in the path of a blind
man,' 'cursed be he who puts an obstacle in the path of a
blind man,' and 'cursed is he who sleeps with his sister,'
'cursed be he who sleeps with his sister' . . . You know
what he said about the commandments.

WHITE BLIND KID

No, no, but, he also says, 'Present yourself honestly,' 'Present yourself honestly, about who you are, 'cause if you don't, I'm gonna make things really bad for you.'

The black blind kid starts beatboxing; the young blind woman tries to rap, starts laughing.

Victor, the albino, starts to rap. Everyone starts to clap and sing along.

CUT TO:

EXT. FRONT LAWN – DAY

Father is having his hair cut by Pearl outside on the lawn. It's sunny out; grandmother watches from the window. Father is expressionless as we hear him in voice-over.

FATHER (V.O.)

Back in the fifties they had this world championship of talking birds. And they sent all these parrots, and beals, it's a starlet type of bird from Borneo, and boy do they speak well. The championship back then was won by a parakeet, a little parakeet, and the parakeet would say, 'Birds are smart, but they cannot speak.' And that really made him a winner. Boy, was that bird good, and you can still buy a record which repeats it, repeats his sentence, 'Birds are smart, but they cannot speak,' and you can teach your own bird. Maybe even dogs are gonna talk one day . . . When we were kids, arriving at the breakfast table we had to say a poem and it went like this . . .

Father recites a poem in German.

And then we were allowed to have our cereals, coffee, whatever there was . . .

CUT TO:

EXT. STREET — DAY

Julien is walking Punky. They walk for a while, cars pass.

    CUT TO:

INT. LIVING ROOM — DAY

Julien is shirtless at the window, watching the mailman across the street. We see the mailman from Julien's POV.

Julien mumbles as the mailman goes about delivering the mail.

JULIEN

Loves me, loves me not. The mailman loves me, loves me not. The mailman loves me, he loves me not . . . I HATE THE MAILMAN!

    CUT TO:

INT. LIVING ROOM — DAY

Julien is sitting in an easy chair, naked except for some underwear and a crucifix around his neck. He talks excitedly, fidgeting, touching himself. We hear a voice off-screen.

VOICE (O.S.)

Hello . . .?

JULIEN
(quietly)

Mom?

VOICE (O.S.)

Hello, Julien?

JULIEN

Mommy!

VOICE (O.S.)

Hi!

JULIEN

Hi, Mommy!

Hi.

JULIEN
Mommy, I can call you mother?

CUT TO:

Pearl. It is she who is on the other end.

PEARL
Hi, Julien, how are you?

JULIEN
I'm doing real good, Mom, I'm fine. I'm a lot better now.
Are you a dietician still, or . . . are you a waitress?

PEARL
No, no, I'm neither one now.

JULIEN
OK, I know, you're a cop, you're a, um, a traffic cop, like a
female police officer of the law.

PEARL
Nope, nope, nope, I'm a dentist now. I fix people's teeth
when they're in pain.

JULIEN
What do you do to dentist, did you go to law school?

PEARL
No, I'm just a basic general dental practitioner. People
come to see me when they have, you know, mouth pain,
and different sorts of ailments, and different sorts of gum
diseases.

JULIEN
You didn't work as a . . . any plastic surgery, there?

PEARL
No, sometimes when people smoke too frequently their
teeth get dirty and me and my staff will whiten them with
special dental tools.

Julien laughs, smiles.

JULIEN

What about my teeth, Mom? I got, I got, um, uh, gold fronts, Chris got me some gold fronts, my little baby brother give me some gold fronts for my birthday, Mom.

PEARL

That was very nice of him.

JULIEN

Yeah, I can eat through, um, apples, and table tops.

They laugh.

PEARL

I don't believe you.

JULIEN

I love you, Mom. I miss you, Mom, I wish you were still here, like when I was a little baby, Mom.

PEARL

Yeah . . . I love you too, Julien . . . And I'm watching you. All those voices you're hearing, those are just friendly voices, no one's out to get you, no one wants to hurt you . . . right? Julien?

JULIEN

I wish you were still here, Mom. Like when I was six, Mom, when I was six you sang 'Frère Jacques.'

They both sing a few bars of the song.

When I was, when I was, when I was six, Chris was four . . . man, Chris was just a little baby, Mom . . . remember Chris, just a little baby? He killed you in the hospital, when they killed you in the hospital, Mom, when they took you away in the hospital and they killed you dead, you remember, Mom, Chris was just a little baby boy.

PEARL

How are your teeth, Julien?

JULIEN

They're, they're OK, they're good.

Julien fidgets with his teeth.

PEARL

Are you brushing daily?

JULIEN

Um, yeah.

PEARL

You have to remember to brush in the crevices, in between the teeth, because that's where the majority of cavities arrive. And floss weekly, at least, the minimum, you must floss once a week.

JULIEN

I promise, I will, I will, I promise, Mom, I'll floss like when you were still alive, when you were still in the house, Mom, I'll floss, I'll floss before you were dead, I'll floss like that, I promise, Mom. OK, I gotta go, I gotta go, OK, I love you, Mom, I love you, Mom, I really love you, I love you soon, I love you soon, you're my best friend, you're my best friend, OK?

PEARL (O.S.)

OK, I love you too, Julien. Bye.

JULIEN

I love you too, Mom.

PEARL

Take good care of your teeth and you'll always be a happy person. OK, Julien? . . . Bye.

JULIEN

Bye, Mom.

PEARL

Bye. I love you, bye.

Julien sits with the phone.

CUT TO:

INT. LIVING ROOM – DAY

Father is doing a parlor trick, listening to the same blues song. He lies on his back, leaps to his feet, and bows.

CUT TO:

INT. DINING ROOM – NIGHT

We see Julien's family from outside through the window. They're having dinner.

Now, inside, no one is talking. Then Julien speaks.

> JULIEN
> So, whoa, whoa, whoa . . . I got, I got, I got a poem . . . wanna hear it?

> PEARL
> OK.

> JULIEN
> Midnight, chaos/Eternity, chaos/Morning, chaos/Noon, chaos/Morning, chaos/Eternity, chaos . . . (*repeated several times*).

The family listens, looks on.

Father becomes annoyed.

> FATHER
> Julien, cut it out.

> JULIEN
> . . . Morning, chaos/Eternity, chaos . . .

> FATHER
> You're repeating chaos, chaos, chaos, you don't even . . . it doesn't even rhyme.

> JULIEN
> It rhymes with chaos, it rhymes with chaos . . .

FATHER

OK, c'mon, c'mon, stop that, that's not a poem.

Julien is visibly distressed.

JULIEN

. . . I'm not finished, midnight . . .

FATHER

What kind of poem is that? C'mon, it doesn't, it doesn't
even rhyme, you repeat chaos, chaos, chaos, and it doesn't
even rhyme.

JULIEN

Chaos . . .

FATHER

How about that?

JULIEN

Right . . . midnight . . .

FATHER

C'mon, shut up, shut up, shut up. I don't like it because
it's so artsy-fartsy. See, I like the real stuff. I like something like, uh, the end of *Dirty Harry*. I saw this *Dirty
Harry* and the end is . . .

He's at a loss for words.

. . . there was this tremendous shoot-out.

Father becomes annoyed with grandmother.

Listen, just listen, Grandmamma, listen, just listen. There
was this shoot-out, uh, Dirty Harry has this bad guy cor-
nered, I mean he was a real, real bad guy. And there's this
tremendous shoot-out, they're really exchanging lots of
fire, they're shooting bullets at each other and they keep
missing. And at the end the bad guy somehow drops his
gun, it's just down there on the bottom. And Harry hovers
over him, and now Harry, I mean, he's really full of con-
tempt, Harry's standing there, he's totally full of con-

tempt, and he says to him: 'We've wasted many of our bullets, do you think there is still a bullet left in your gun?' And he says to him: 'You know, now you've gotta ask yourself a question: "Do I feel lucky?"' Then, at that moment, the bad guy lunges for his gun, raises it and it just goes 'click.' He hasn't got a bullet left, and Harry blasts him away, just blasts him into a river, blasts him in, knocks him off his feet and blasts him away . . .

The family listens awkwardly.

So that's, that's good stuff. I truly like that. I don't like the artsy-fartsy thing, I think I hated his poem.

Julien sits, silent.

CUT TO:

INT. LIVING ROOM – DAY

Chris and father are in the living room. Father holds a glass and a plate. Chris is balanced on his arms above the ground. Grandmother looks on from the couch.

FATHER
Now, Chris, I'd like to see you do that.

Chris sits down.

You see, it's all balance. You're really balancing. You know what I had to do when I was a ski-jumper, when I was your age, we had a really, really, mean, nasty trick to do. We put a cigarette on the ground, just like that . . .

Father sets down a plate and puts a cigarette end-up on it.

And a glass of water . . .

Father puts a glass on the ground about three feet from the cigarette, stands on it with one foot, tries to balance.

And you just gotta step on this glass, and you have to pick it up, you have to balance, you have to pick it up with your mouth without falling, it's really, really a tough one.

Father steps off the glass, gets back on.

> CHRIS

You could do it?

> FATHER

No, I don't think I could do it any more, but usually I was able to do it.

He tries, falls.

It's all balance.

He tries, falls again.

Agh.

Father sits down next to Chris on the couch.

> CHRIS

Did you ever do it?

> FATHER

Yeah, it was difficult, but I could do it. I really wanted to be a champion, I really wanted to be good.

Chris gets up to make a try.

He's gonna do it, Grandmamma.

Chris leans over, gets close to the cigarette.

All right, all right.

Chris gets the cigarette in his mouth, then he falls over. Father pats him on the back.

Yeah, yeah, yeah, that's good. You're gonna do it.

Father gets up and walks around.

In two or three weeks you are gonna do that.

> CHRIS

I just did it.

FATHER

Yeah, but you fell, you, you see, you've gotta raise up again and smoke the cigarette, that's a proud man who smokes a cigarette like that.

CHRIS

I don't smoke.

FATHER

Well, you'll learn it.

CUT TO:

INT. HOME FOR THE BLIND – NIGHT

A party is being held for the blind kids at the home.

Balloons and streamers are everywhere, people are dressed in costumes, smiling, dancing.

A man in a sombrero plays the organ and sings 'My Bonny Lies Over the Ocean' in a hammy voice; everyone sings along.

SOMBRERO MAN

My Bonnie lies over the ocean/My Bonnie lies over the sea/My Bonnie lies over the ocean/Oh bring my poor Bonnie to me/Bring back, bring back/Bring back my Bonnie to me . . .

A woman in the crowd smiles.

WOMAN

That's my son up there!

The albino from the earlier meeting sits, smiling, wearing earmuffs.

Julien sits with Christie.

He stretches it out for the finale.

SOMBRERO MAN

My Bonnie lies over the ocean/My Bonnie doesn't lie over me!

Someone yells, 'Let's party!'

A guy in a bad tux smokes, ten, twenty cigarettes at once.

Someone yells, 'Great act for blind people.'

He then eats the cigarettes, along with a few handfuls of kleenex.

CIGARETTE MAN

Well, that's it. Thank you very much.

Cheering all around.

SOMBRERO MAN

All riiiiight!

The white blind kid from earlier gets up to the dancefloor with some assistance.

SOMEONE IN CROWD

David!

More cheering.

SOMBRERO MAN

All right!

The sombrero man plays the organ again, singing while the white blind kid dances.

Amen, amen, amen, amen . . .

Everybody gets up and dances, shouting, 'We don't need no music!' over and over.

The party becomes a blur.

CUT TO:

EXT. BUS STOP – DAY

Julien stands at a bus stop with Christie. She has ice skates around her neck.

CUT TO:

INT. BATHROOM – DAY

Julien and Christie are in a bathroom, bathed in red light. Julien is washing her feet while she sings James Brown's 'I Feel Good.'

> CHRISTIE
> I feel good, na na na na na na na/I knew that I would, na na na na na na na/I feel good, na na na na na na na/I knew that I would, na na na na na na na/So good, na na/So good, na na/I got you, na na na na na na/I feel nice, na na na na na na/Like sugar and spice, na na na na na na na . . .

Julien laughs, sings along.

> JULIEN
> That's my favorite song, I love that song.

> CHRISTIE
> What song?

> JULIEN
> That song: 'Na na na na na na, I feel tosh . . .'

Christie laughs loudly.

> That's a brilliant song.

> CHRISTIE
> I think one day when my feet break apart I'm gonna need new feet. Or I'm gonna have to sew these feet back on.

Julien roars with laughter again.

> JULIEN
> I met a man, I met a man that was really clean like me and he said, 'If you wanna, if you wanna have clean feet, you've gotta listen to clean tapes.'

Christie laughs again.

> CHRISTIE
> That tickles!

JULIEN

I'm sorry.

CHRISTIE

Ah, you don't have to be sorry. It feels good.

JULIEN

Does this tickle with my brush?

Julien tickles her foot with the brush.

CHRISTIE
(laughing)

Yes.

They both laugh some more.

All my boyfriends are dead, and you're gonna die too, maybe too, Julien.

JULIEN

I died before, you know, I died before.

CHRISTIE

I'm gonna die before I die, I'm gonna make a high dive, and then as soon as I land in the water I'm gonna die.

JULIEN

Really?

CHRISTIE

Yeah, I'm gonna die from the 2,000-meter board and then, I'm gonna fall, fall, fall, until I fall in the water and then I'm gonna die.

CUT TO:

INT. – DAY

Grainy image of ice skater in black and white. Opera plays.

CUT TO:

EXT. BACK PORCH — DAY

A series of stills of Pearl. She is outside, wearing a ratty pink coat and a skirt.

Pearl plays with the hose, jumps on a pogo stick. We hear her in voice-over as she lists possible names for her baby.

> PEARL (V.O.)
> Lillian, David, Sylvia, Simon, Casey, Sasha, Scott, Joshua, Jezebel, Harold, Harry, Caroline, Sarah, Sylvia . . .

She climbs onto the porch.

> Simon, Lewis, Michael, Walter, Brendan, Olivia, Ethan, Eleanor, Gloria, or Ellen. Those are my favorites so far.

CUT TO:

INT. LIVING ROOM — DAY

Chris stretches, wearing his wrestling outfit. Father and grandmother sit on the couch. Father has drawn another moustache on his face.

Julien runs in, arms in the air. He is wearing bikini underwear, one of Pearl's bras, black socks, and a Japanese handkerchief. He's jumping around exuberantly.

Pearl laughs.

> FATHER (O.S.)
> What sort of outfit is that, come on, this is ridiculous.

Julien keeps jumping.

> JULIEN
> Papa papa papa, listen. Julien the Jamming Jabber, Julien the Jamming Jabber.

> PEARL
> OK, Julien the Jamming Jabber, stay in your corner . . .

Julien runs to Pearl and puts his arms around her waist.

. . . and Chris, you get in your corner. C'mon we're gonna
start the match, now, c'mon.

CHRIS

I wanted, I wanted to wrestle for real.

PEARL

He's gonna wrestle for real.
(*to Julien*)
Are you gonna wrestle for real?

JULIEN

You ready? You ready?

PEARL

Yeah, you're gonna wrestle Chris. And Chris, what's your
name, what's your wrestling name?

CHRIS

Chris.

PEARL

No, but you have to have a name, you know, like a cos-
tume, a name.

CHRIS

It's Chris.

Julien starts yelling, runs toward Chris.

JULIEN

Julien the Jamming Jabber! Julien the Jamming Jabber!

CHRIS
(*ignoring Julien*)
It's real wrestling, my name's Chris, it's real wrestling.

PEARL

OK, OK, OK, all right . . .

CHRIS

Come on . . .

FATHER

Get serious.

PEARL

In the center of the ring, Julien, in the center of the ring.
And shake, let's shake . . .

Julien shakes and jumps around.

Pearl tries to calm him.

No, no, no, shake hands. Shake hands.

CHRIS

Be serious, be serious.

Chris and Julien shake hands.

PEARL

I'm listening, I'm gonna watch them, OK?

CHRIS

Be serious.

JULIEN

I know, I know, I know.

PEARL

You ready for the fight?

Chris waits for the count, concentrating.

You ready? One . . . you ready? One, two . . .

Chris and Julien shake along with her count.

Three! Wrestle! Come on!

Pearl cheers and watches from the side.

JULIEN

Bring it on!

CHRIS

Come on, come on!

Chris easily pushes Julien into the couch.

Wrestle me, man.

PEARL
(*to Julien*)

Grab him, grab him, get him to the ground! Get him to the ground! Come on, Julien!

Chris easily pushes Julien around; Julien doesn't really fight back.

JULIEN

Julien the Jamming Jabber, Julien the Jamming Jabber.

Julien falls into the couch, next to his father.

FATHER

Come on, get into the fight.

Everyone shouts, coaxing Julien. Julien reaches for the banana his father is eating. His father pushes him away.

Not now, not when you are fighting.

Chris is now on top of Julien, forcing him to the ground. Pearl is right on top of them.

PEARL

Oh, he's got 'em, oh, they're goin' down! Oh, he's got 'em.

Chris pins Julien.

Come on, Chris, get him, Chris! Come on, Julien, you have to fight harder! Come on!

Julien escapes, gets up.

JULIEN

Julien the Jamming Jabber, Julien the Jamming Jabber!

CHRIS

Get serious.

Chris wrestles Julien to the ground yet again.

Get serious, Julien.

PEARL

You can fight back, come on.

Julien escapes again, raises his arms triumphantly. Chris is obviously getting angry.

JULIEN

Bring it on!

Chris starts shoving Julien. Julien looks upset.

CHRIS

You told me you'd take it seriously, you told me you'd take it serious.

CUT TO:

Julien pinned on the floor. Chris's face is inches from Julien's.

PEARL

Julien, fight back, Julien, fight back.

CHRIS

Come on, come on, fight back! Come on, fuckin' fight back, man!

Meanwhile, Pearl has been counting while Julien's been pinned.

PEARL

. . . three! You're out!

Julien flips Chris over, tries to pin him.

He's up again!

Just as quickly, Chris pins Julien again.

Pissed off, Chris jumps up. Julien is whining like he's been hurt.

CHRIS

Cut it out! What is wrong with you?! God-fucking-damnit!

Pearl watches, doesn't speak.

Father picks up his banana peel off the floor and throws it down again.

FATHER

Disqualified for bad behavior!

Julien throws the bra he was wearing onto the ground.

JULIEN

I'm never gonna wear that again.

Julien wanders outside after Chris, who has started walking down the street.

FATHER (O.S.)

I found it very, very shitty, actually.

Julien runs after Chris and catches up to him, tries to bring him back.

Chris turns back to the house, ignoring Julien's apologies as they both walk back.

JULIEN

Come on . . . OK, OK, OK? I won't, I won't, I won't hit you . . . I didn't wanna, I didn't wanna hurt you, Chris . . . I didn't wanna hurt you, I didn't wanna hurt you, like . . . put you in the hospital, like, put you in the hospital, like Mommy . . .

Chris turns, shoves Julien back.

CHRIS

Just fuckin' act fuckin' normal for a second and fuckin' take it serious.

Chris turns and keeps walking back to the house. Julien follows.

JULIEN

Sorry sorry sorry.

CUT TO:

INT. BATHROOM — NIGHT

Julien stands in his bathroom wearing only his underwear.

Opera plays in the background.

He spins around, raising his arms and legs. He seems to be attempting a variation on the ice-skating tricks that we've seen before.

Julien starts taking pills from bottles in the medicine cabinet.

CUT TO:

EXT. STREET — DAY

Pearl spins in the street, holding an umbrella. She sings a cheerful little melody.

CUT TO:

INT. HOME FOR THE BLIND — DAY

Christie dancing in a studio. She spins happily as a melody plays on a nearby piano.

CUT TO:

EXT. STREET — DAY

Pearl dancing again; we are seeing her from above, from a window.

CUT TO:

INT. HOME FOR THE BLIND — DAY

Christie dances as Julien watches.

CUT TO:

EXT. STREET — DAY

Pearl spins, twirling her umbrella.

CUT TO:

INT. HOME FOR THE BLIND — DAY

Christie again, dancing to 'Chopsticks.' Julien joins her as they both twirl around the room.

CUT TO:

INT. HOSPITAL — DAY

Two old women sit on a couch in a sterile hospital waiting room, watching Julien mop the floor.

One woman sports what appears to be a thick moustache. Her head is wrapped in gauze.

The other is wearing a blue sack over her head, with eyeholes cut out. She occasionally makes little grunting noises.

Julien mops, oblivious.

They lift their feet so he can mop under the couch.

    CUT TO:

INT. CHURCH — DAY

Julien and his family are in a black Baptist church.

The reverend is singing/sermonizing, and people are on their feet, clapping, nodding.

Julien stands, watches the reverend, clapping and praying.

              REVEREND
There is no forgiveness of sins, amen, and so by the blood of Jesus, we are forgiven, Amen . . .

Julien is lost in prayer.

His family looks on.

. . . that the blood of Jesus Christ, Amen, must cleanse us, Amen . . . when I have done wrong and my sins catch up with me, Jesus, Amen, when the Lord looks at me, he sees the blood of Jesus, Amen . . .

Julien takes this all in, looks around, listens. His siblings listen intently.

. . . And I'm glad to know that Jesus paid the price. He wrested us, Amen, from the very gates of hell.

Everybody claps.

I don't know about you, but I'm glad that I've been washed in his blood, I'm glad to know that I've been redeemed by the blood of the lamb. The blood has made my spirit clean. And his blood has wrote my name above . . .

Everyone nods.

I don't know about you but I was a sinner one day but I'm glad that I brought Jesus from it. Amen, and I've been set free today. Amen, I don't know about you but I'm glad that we can sing this song: 'What Can Wash Away My Sins?' We have heard from heaven today, the Lord has stopped by to visit us. You know, and I'm so glad of one thing, and I be getting ready to go, and I feel good . . .

Julien rests his head on the pew. He begins to cry.

. . . 'cause I know that can't nobody do me like Jesus. And if you don't mind, we gonna do just a little bit of that great song, and we'll be on our way home.

The reverend and the congregation begin to sing 'Can't Nobody Do Me Like Jesus.'

Julien cries, claps, dances.

The whole church sings and claps along. Julien's father plays with a small black child. Julien continues to clap and dance, more exuberantly, desperately.

CUT TO:

INT. KITCHEN – DAY

A series of very fast jump cuts. Chris and Julien are in the kitchen.

Julien is throwing bacon at a cowering Chris, who whimpers.

Julien pushes Chris around, shoves bacon in his face. Chris doesn't fight back.

Julien cooks some bacon, puts it in a bowl on the floor.

He orders Chris on all fours to eat it.

CUT TO:

EXT. STREET — NIGHT

Julien walks in the middle of the street, cars passing, as spare guitar plays in the background.

CUT TO:

INT. PEARL'S ROOM — NIGHT

Pearl is playing her harp while Julien looks on from the floor.

Father plucks at the harp aggressively.

Julien is enjoying the music.

> FATHER
> Julien, why don't you tell your sister that she's a dilettante. She's never gonna learn to play this harp. She's a dilettante and she's a slut.

> JULIEN
> (*robotically*)
> You're a diletent, and you're a slut, and you're never gonna learn to play the harp.

Suddenly father smacks at the harp strings, knocking it out of Pearl's hands.

> FATHER
> I can't take this any longer!

Julien shrieks, stands up, afraid.

> I can't stand this any longer, I might accidentally step on this here.

> JULIEN AND PEARL
> No!

> FATHER
> Come on, don't try to defend your sister, you'll just look stupid.

Father pushes at Julien.

JULIEN

I . . .

FATHER

You're just stupid!

Julien starts.

You look so stupid, you look utterly, and completely, and irrevocably stupid. You're so stupid, if I were so stupid . . .

JULIEN

I'm not stupid . . .

FATHER

If I were so stupid I would slap my own face.

JULIEN

Ah ha ha ha! Well, I'm not even stupid.

Julien starts slapping himself.

Well, I'm not even stupid like that! Well, I'm not even stupid like that.

Julien keeps slapping himself; father is growing angrier.

FATHER
(*to Pearl*)

Tell him to slap his face.

PEARL

No.

JULIEN

Well, I'm not even stupid like that.

FATHER

He should slap his face.

PEARL

No. Julien, relax. Don't listen to what he says. Julien, no.

FATHER

Slap your face.

JULIEN

No, no! I ain't gotta be stupid like that!

PEARL

No, Julien!

Julien is becoming increasingly agitated. Pearl tries to help. He keeps hitting himself.

FATHER

Slap your face, slap your face!

JULIEN

I ain't gonna be stupid like that, I ain't gonna be stupid like that, I ain't gonna be stupid like that . . .

FATHER

TELL HIM TO SLAP HIS FACE!

Julien, lying on the bed, wags his finger at father.

Slap your face, you should slap your face.

Julien keeps shaking his head.

Just, you might even wake up, you should slap your face. If I were as stupid, I would slap my own face. Just tell him to slap his face.

JULIEN

I'm really stupid.

Pearl sits on the bed, Julien is beginning to lose it.

FATHER
(*to Pearl*)

Why don't you tell him to slap his own face?

JULIEN

Pearl?

FATHER

Just slap your face.

JULIEN

Pearl.

FATHER

Just slap your face, I'll turn my back.

JULIEN

Pearl . . . Dad?

FATHER

I'll turn my back and he's gonna start . . .

JULIEN

Dad?

FATHER

. . . start slapping his face.

JULIEN

Dad.

FATHER

You are gonna do it, because you will wake up . . . SLAP.
YOUR. FACE!

JULIEN

Slap my face?

Father turns, roaring. Julien cowers.

FATHER

SLAP YOUR FACE!

Julien starts slapping his face again.

(*to Pearl*)
Tell him to slap it harder. Tell him to slap it harder.

JULIEN

I can't, Dad, it hurts.

FATHER

Slap it harder.

JULIEN

I can't, it really hurts.

Julien starts hitting himself harder, faster.

FATHER

Maybe you'll become more intelligent.

JULIEN

Can it hurt me, Pop? Can it hurt me, Pop?

FATHER

Yeah.

JULIEN

Can it hurt me, Pop?

FATHER

Yeah.

JULIEN

Can it hurt me, Pop?

FATHER

Why don't you lie down? Why don't you lie down and keep on slapping your face?

Julien keeps hitting himself, over and over.

Just keep on slapping your face. And you take this fucking harp . . .

Julien kneels down, keeps slapping himself.

Slap your face!

JULIEN

OK, OK, OK . . .

FATHER
(*to Pearl*)

Tell him to slap his face. You sing, you sing the song . . .

JULIEN

OK, OK, OK . . .

FATHER

You shut up, you sing the song.

Father roughly plucks at the harp.

Julien keeps babbling, slapping himself.

You pluck this fucking thing.

Father turns away from Julien.

Julien slaps himself even harder.

You slap your face. I just can't take it any longer.

Julien starts punching himself in the head, breaking down.

I just can't take it any longer.

JULIEN

Can it hurt me, Pop? Can it hurt me?

FATHER (O.S.)

Just sing the song. Just sing, sing the song.

JULIEN

Can it hurt me? Hurt me, hurt me, Pop?

Pearl puts her arms around Julien, trying to comfort him.

Julien hits himself, curls into a ball, starts to totally break down.

Father plucks at the harp again off-screen.

FATHER

Come on, sing the song.

JULIEN

Hurt me? Can it hurt me, Pop? Can it hurt me, Pop? Can it hurt me, Pop?

Julien is getting worse; father keeps asking him to sing. Pearl is unable to calm Julien.

Julien collapses to the floor, crying, shaking, babbling.

Pearl is on top of him, holding him and whispering to calm him.

Can it hurt me, Pop? Just close your eyes . . . just close . . .
where, where, blood has been spilled . . . life is life, life is
life, show Jesus flowers and collect his blood, show Jesus
flowers and collect his blood. Blood is life, life is the
blood.

*Julien keeps moaning, but he starts to calm down. Eventually, he
stops.*

CUT TO:

INT. HOCKEY RINK – DAY

Blurs of people skating, music.

*People are skating, Julien is sitting on a bench next to the rink talk-
ing to a small Hassidic boy, Ricky.*

*Julien holds a slipper that has a skate blade glued onto it; Ricky has
an ice-cream cone.*

RICKY

Sorry, they're stupid little, little pieces of crap that are
glued together, that if you fall, if you fall in them you'll
die, and . . .

JULIEN

No, no, no, you're not gonna die, you're not gonna die . . .

Ricky eats his ice cream, ignoring Julien.

. . . because these are the two, two safest things in the
world. You, you got, you got double, double-blade, double-
blade technology from . . . from ice skates, and you got,
you got the safest thing in the world, which is a flip-flop,
and you glue 'em together, and you got something which is
more secure, and you got shoes you can wear in the house,
you got shoes you can wear in the park, you got shoes you
can wear on the ice rink . . .

Pearl and Christie are sitting nearby. Christie is looking at Pearl's belly.

On the glass in front of them, we see the reflections of figure skaters performing tricks.

PEARL

It's getting big, huh?

CHRISTIE

Your baby's due in two months?

PEARL

Uh, yep, two months, in two months' time it's due . . .
How do you think the future for the baby looks?

CHRISTIE

Bright.

Pearl laughs, imitates the blind girl's tone.

PEARL

Bright?

CHRISTIE

Bright as the sun.

PEARL

Whoah.

A skater dressed in white spins on the ice.

CHRISTIE

How come everybody, um, comes out of their mother's
stomach as a baby?

PEARL

Because, well, they have to be so small to fit in there
because there's not a lot of room.

CHRISTIE

Yeah, they can't just come out as eleven- or twelve-year-
olds 'cause that would be really, really big.

Pearl laughs.

. . . and *so* painful.

PEARL

Ooh, could you imagine? That would be horrible.

Return to Julien and Ricky.

JULIEN

Ten bucks. Ten bucks and your ice cream, five bucks, you, and the ice cream.

RICKY

Ten bucks? I wouldn't pay, I wouldn't pay a dime for those.

JULIEN

You . . . I swear, swear, swear . . .

RICKY

You probably just, you know I could make those myself, I just take one of my sandals and put, and put two blades on top.

More ice skaters.

You think those are actually gonna make you stand up?

JULIEN

No, no, no, no, no, I don't even . . .

RICKY

Just leave me alone, I don't want 'em! OK? Period, I don't want them.

JULIEN

Ricky, Ricky, Ricky, you gotta trust me. What you want with my flippy-flips . . .

RICKY

You're getting on my nerves. If you don't want, if you don't want to stop, then I'm going to have to curse you out in Yiddish, OK?

Return to Pearl and Christie.

CHRISTIE

You know what I used to think?

PEARL

What?

CHRISTIE

I used to think I could see a lot, but I found out that I couldn't see very much.

PEARL

Oh . . .

CHRISTIE

That my vision was almost slim to none.

PEARL

Really?

CHRISTIE

I thought I could almost see totally.

PEARL

So if nobody had ever told you then you would maybe never even know.

CHRISTIE

No. I thought I could really see, like almost normal sight, but I found out I'm not even close.

Another skater spins; we follow her. Strange music plays.

We return to Julien and Ricky. Ricky is waving his ice-cream cone threateningly.

RICKY

If you don't, if you don't leave me alone I'm gonna smear this all over your face.

JULIEN

Can I get a little, can I get a little . . .

RICKY

No. You're not gonna have it. You're not gonna have it

period. Not even if . . . if you leave me alone, I'll throw it
on the floor, and I'll let you lick it off the floor.

*The music continues to hum in the background. We return to Pearl
and Christie.*

> PEARL

Sometimes I wish I was deaf.

> CHRISTIE

Why?

> PEARL

I don't know, I think the world is just too loud . . .

Quick blur of ice skaters.

Back to Julien and Ricky.

Ricky is increasingly annoyed.

> RICKY

How about you go home, and uh, go to the bathroom,
make in the toilet, and then eat some shit?

People ice skating.

Pearl and Christie can be seen ice skating in the crowd.

> CHRISTIE

I can glide like this.

> PEARL

Oh, no, no, no, no, no . . .

> CHRISTIE

Why not, it's fun.

> PEARL

Slow down, slow down, Christie.

Now we are closer to them, following them as they skate.

> CHRISTIE

I've got you. Trust me.

PEARL

Let's not go crazy here.

CHRISTIE

We can still have fun.

PEARL

We can still have fun, but I don't wanna go fast.

CHRISTIE

Ooh.

PEARL

You maybe need a better skater to hold your hand when you try tricks . . . Oh, no, my skate's undone. My lace is undone, I'm gonna have to go to the wall.

Pearl and Christie sit at the wall while Pearl ties her laces.

CHRISTIE

We don't want you tripping and falling.

They skate some more.

A blur of other skaters.

PEARL

No, no, no, don't go too fast. Wait, wait, wait, wait, I'm way behind you here.

Pearl notices some other skaters.

Hey, these girls are really good, maybe one of them will skate with you. Do you wanna skate with one of these girls?

CHRISTIE

Yes.

Pearl almost falls.

PEARL

Whoah . . .

Christie goes off with one of the girls.

CHRISTIE

This is really good.

SKATING GIRL I

You having fun?

CHRISTIE

Yes.

SKATING GIRL I

That's good. You feel the wind in your hair?

Back to Julien.

He happily watches Pearl from the benches.

She spins on the ice, does tricks like the ice skaters we've seen earlier.

Christie skates with the other girl; things become blurry.

Close-up of Pearl as she skates and spins around on the ice. She smiles.

Christie skates by Pearl.

Close-up of Christie as she skates, a smile on her face.

Julien still watching Pearl.

Pearl falls forward, landing on her stomach.

She screams, clutching her belly.

Julien leaps off the bench.

JULIEN

Fire!

Pearl lies on the ice, wailing.

Julien runs to her side.

Fire! Fire!

He holds her, moaning.

Christie skates alone at the other end of the ice.

Ricky sings in Hebrew as Christie skates some more.

CUT TO:

INT. HOSPITAL — DAY

Close-up of Pearl's face. She is in a lot of pain.

Doctors are rushing her down the hall of the hospital as she wails.

DOCTOR I
Get her in carefully now.

A doctor leans over Pearl to examine her.

DOCTOR 2
How are you feeling now?

PEARL
It hurts so much . . .

DOCTOR 2
Where does it hurt? Show me with one finger where it
hurts.

PEARL
Right there . . .

DOCTOR 2
OK.
(*to the other doctor*)
What's the story here?

Pearl's screams are getting louder.

Was there any bleeding, any hemorrhage?

DOCTOR I
No, nothing.

DOCTOR 2
OK.

PEARL
Help me . . .

DOCTOR 2

You're gonna be OK, you just . . . try and relax.

DOCTOR 1

Blood pressure in the field looks stable.

DOCTOR 2

OK.

Chris arrives at the emergency room with Julien trailing behind. Both are upset, speechless.

They watch outside through the window.

Pearl's screams are audible through the window as the two of them look in.

Julien is crying.

CUT TO:

INT. JULIEN'S HOUSE – DAY

Through a chandelier, we can see Julien's father.

He is wearing his gas mask and dancing to opera, dancing as if he had a partner.

CUT TO:

INT. HOSPITAL – DAY

Back in the hospital, Julien and Chris are still waiting.

A nurse leaves with the miscarried fetus and walks down the hall.

Julien follows.

The nurse puts the fetus down on a metal table.

Julien enters.

JULIEN

Excuse me, miss? Do you think I could possibly see the baby for a moment?

NURSE

Oh, I'm sorry, the baby's dead.

JULIEN

I understand, I understand, but, um, it's my baby. I'd just like, I'd just like to hold him before you put the baby away, can I just hold the baby?

The nurse considers, then gives Julien the baby.

He holds it, looks at it intently.

Julien runs out of the room, runs down the hall and out some stairs.

CUT TO:

EXT. STREET — DAY

Julien carries the baby down a mostly empty, dirty street. He picks up a blanket and wraps the baby.

CUT TO:

EXT. BUS STOP — DAY

Julien, expressionless, gets on a bus.

He sits down, cradling the baby, stroking it.

Someone next to him is visibly uncomfortable, but mostly he sits ignored, holding the baby, rocking back and forth. Stop after stop goes by.

People start moving away from Julien. He stares out the window.

CUT TO:

EXT. JULIEN'S STREET — LATE AFTERNOON

Julien walks down his street, still cradling the baby.

CUT TO:

INT. JULIEN'S HOUSE — DAY

He enters his house.

Nobody is home; he goes upstairs to his room and sits on his bed.

He holds the baby, looks at its face, touches his face to it.

Julien slowly pulls himself and the baby under his covers.

He sits under the sheets, rocking back and forth, whispering over and over.

> JULIEN
> Daddy's baby, Daddy's baby, Daddy's baby, Daddy's baby . . .

His eyes stare straight ahead.

Eventually he stops whispering, stops moving.

FADE TO BLACK.

CUT TO:

INT. — DAY

Opera plays again.

A blurry, grainy image of another figure skater.

She skates in slow motion, spinning and jumping.